A BOY'S LIFE

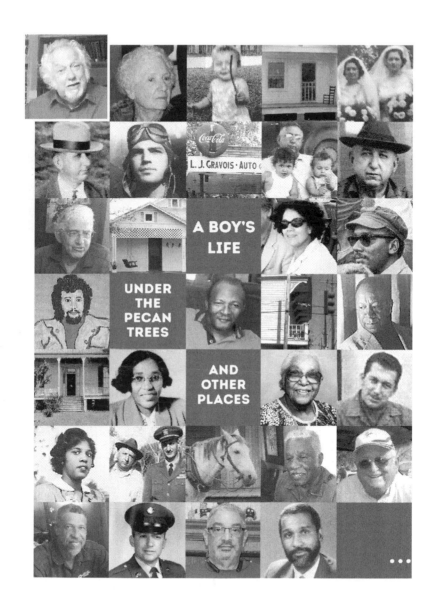

A BOY'S
LIFE

UNDER
THE
PECAN
TREES

AND
OTHER
PLACES

Colin Gravois

A BOY'S LIFE

UNDER THE PECAN TREES
AND OTHER PLACES

Published by Les Éditions du Beauvallon
Paris, France

First printing April 2021
Second printing February 2022
Library of Congress Cataloging-in-Publication Data

*****

1. Gravois, Colin, 1942 –
2. *A Boy's Life Under the Pecan Trees and Other Places*

*****

Cover design by Gilles Arira
from a 1946 photo of a Sunday outing at Tony Gravois's
hunting camp on *Lac Des Allemands* in Vacherie, Louisiana.

Cover photo credit: Helen Reulet Gravois

*****

Composition and layout: Gilles Arira, Paris

This book is dedicated to
Helen Eugenie Reulet Gravois

CONTENTS

A good man doubles the length of his existence. To have lived so as to look back with pleasure on our past existence is to live twice.

Marcus Valerius Martialis

* * * * * * * *

In the journey of life some are left behind, because they are naturally feeble and slow, some because they miss the way, and many because they leave it by choice, instead of pressing onward with a steady pace, delight themselves with momentary deviations, turn aside to pluck every flower, and repose in every shade.

Dr. Samuel Johnson

* * * * * * * *

Always run towards your dreams.

J. Victor Reulet

Foreword

There are many ways to tell a life.

I grew up in the 1940s and 50s in the small rural settlement of Vacherie, Louisiana, about 50 miles up the Mississippi River from New Orleans. That particular community, including my very large extended family, provided me with a long list of memorable characters and events, a few of which I recall for you in this book.

In wondering why I remember some specific moments I evoke, I've concluded that it's a person's humanity that most impresses me, when all is said and done. (Or, in the case of one of my portraits — Père Delnom — his lack of humanity.) There is something radiant about a human being who has both the intelligence and the heart to rise above near-impossible circumstances — the travesty of segregation, for example. I learned a great deal about humankind by listening to the stories of Black friends in my community.

Most importantly, I'm descended from people who were avid readers. Who were curious about the world. This inspired my curiosity, and is the reason why I wanted to travel to other countries and explore the wider world myself, ending up settling in France in 1968. From the backwoods of Louisiana to Paris is a long distance, by any system of measurement. But even living in a city considered one of the most sophisticated in the world, I have never once lost the pride of having my roots in the soil of the American south, and in Vacherie. Nor have I lost admiration for the many inspiring people I encountered there — whether Black or White, family, friend, or stranger.

Other stories in this book include reports I sent home from my Army days in Germany; my visit in 1967 to the original Reulet homestead in southern France; a eulogy or two of people I've loved dearly; odds and ends; and short profiles of a half-dozen African American friends who helped me understand what it was like to grow up Black during segregation.

I include what I'm calling my "Black stories" for some of the people who will read this book who still have no idea what African Americans had to face every single day in the South. I sincerely hope they will learn something from hearing first-hand what their Black neighbors were going through when the society we lived in at that time, in southern Louisiana, was in the throes of Jim Crow segregation. This alone would make my effort to share these stories worthwhile.

Take care — and happy reading.

Cut Store, gone but not forgotten. The Falgoust Brothers' general store, around 1915, where my grandfather Pépère Victor Reulet had his first job after his studies at Soulé College in New Orleans. The upper rear part of the store was demolished at one time ("cut away" from the main building, as they said), and it was from then on known as "Cut Store." It closed around 1950.

IN THE BEGINNING

A Baby Arrives

I was born in the middle of a cattle drive.

The day I made my entrance into this world, June 3, 1942, was the day my grandfather, Pépère Victor Reulet, had his cows vaccinated by the County Agent. Both events took place on the same property. Pépère had scheduled this date some weeks previously without knowing, of course, that my mother would be giving birth to me at the same time.

Earlier that day, Elie "Boy" Isom, Pépère's handyman from across the road, rounded up the cattle in the woods and pastures and drove them to the front part of the property, where they could be more easily lassoed and restrained. The house I was born in was situated right in the middle of Pépère's vast front yard, where all the action with the cattle was taking place. Inside, Mama was giving birth to me; outside, the local cow pokes had their hands full with the quadrupeds.

Aunt Marie, who had observed both operations closely, described that dramatic moment to me on many occasions. She said Vacherie was in the middle of a summer heat wave and that the men were sweating hard, chasing the cattle around and around all over the yard, and that every now and then there was a loud thump on the outside of Mama's room when one of the cows bumped into the house. For several hours, it was complete pandemonium. Raucous noises and shouting came from both inside and out, culminating at 2:10 p.m., when I let out my primal scream.

Aunt Marie recounted how Pépère was supervising everything from the back steps of his home, which had a clear view of both the yard and of our house, about 40 feet away. She assured me he was far more preoccupied with the event taking place indoors. Marie described the moment when he heard his new grandson let out that first cry: Pépère burst into tears and put his head in his hands. He was a sentimental, sensitive sort, Pépère was. After that overflow of emotion, he turned his attention back to the operations in the yard with renewed vigour.

*

Pépère Victor on his back steps, like during the cattle drive.

The town where I was born, Vacherie, Louisiana, was a French-speaking community about 50 miles upriver from New Orleans on the West Bank of the Mississippi. It was founded by Germans and later populated by new French arrivals. Yes, Germans — brought to Louisiana by the Mississippi Company, a French concern formed to develop the colony. A few years later, the company crashed in a bankruptcy scandal known as "The Mississippi Bubble" (see *Vacherie, a Brief History*).

After they were married in September 1939, my parents rented a "starter house," where my sister, Lael, was born. It was called The Smith House, and is still referred to as such. Located on the Vacherie Road, it's about half-way between the railroad tracks and the Mississippi River levee. The sturdy red-brick structure is still standing today and in a good state of repair. In those days, it was situated next to a yellow shotgun-style building that later became the R.P. Drugstore. That building did not age well and was demolished a few years ago, shortly before it would have crashed to the ground under its own weight!

My parents' wedding, September 1939.
From left: Firmin Steib, Leonard Gravois, Paul and Helen,
Bernice Reulet, Claire Gravois.

My parents built a new house quickly — as a solution to paying rent — with plans to move it to a permanent location once they could afford a piece of land, a goal that took about seven years to achieve.

Our house was just beyond the pecan trees toward the back of a huge yard. Pépère's house (where Marjorie lives today) was to the east and Aunt Marie's (today Dick's) was to the west. Three towering pecan trees stood in the front part of the property, between the two large houses. Our house was about equidistant from each of the others and set a bit to the back of the huge trees. Growing up, it felt to me like I had three homes, which was a good feeling to have as a little boy. I could spend time in any one of them, bathing in the love and affection of my extended family.

I spent so much time under those pecan trees in Pépère's yard, starting with my first baby steps and going all the way through adulthood, that I like to say I was born right there, under those big leafy branches. And I'm not very far off. I came into this world only a few feet from the shade cast by the trees' most southern leaves.

Our house was built by Uncle Bertrand Reulet ("Beel"), Pépère's brother, and his partner on that job, John Lasserre. I know Beel was a skilled carpenter, but I never knew "Jone" had done carpentry work until Mama mentioned a few years ago that he'd worked with Bertrand on the house. By the time I got to know this fine man well, he was a retired gentleman. In summer, I'd see him whiling away the hot afternoons with his elderly pals, under the tree near Terrance Oubre's store in the Front Lane. He always greeted me with a wide smile. Jone Lasserre was a good man.

*

The sawing and shaping of the lumber for the house was done by hand, and it took "all" of two months to complete the job. (Imagine what they could have accomplished with power tools.) Added to the long hours of labor, the pay was nothing to brag about. Beel only made $1.25 per day! He told Mama, "As your uncle, I'll make you a special price. But my partner

Our favorite spot under the pecan trees, September 1942.
Pépère Victor, Lael, and me.

on this job, Jone Lasserre, refuses to go below $1.75 a day. Can you and Paul work with that?"

They could.

The total cost for the house was $2,000, excluding labor. My parents paid $1,200 cash with an $800 mortgage from the Frost Lumber Company in Thibodaux, which also supplied the building materials. The monthly payments were $15.

Our new house was box-shaped, a little longer than wide; the outside walls were painted white and made of fitted weatherboards, called locally, "voliches." It had a roof of galvanized corrugated tin, with no insulation between the roof and the ceiling. Summers were extremely hot with this type of construction.

It had two bedrooms on one side separated by a bathroom. The living room and kitchen were in the other half. There was a front porch which gave out onto the yard and the pecan trees. The porch offered us a lovely view and was a fine place

Our new house in the big yard where the cattle drive was held.

to spend the evenings in rocking chairs, watching the world go by.

When the house was being remodelled for the first time in 1949, the carpenter discovered a message written by Uncle Beel on the backside of a weatherboard. It described the job, noting the builders' names and the date — a time capsule of sorts, waiting to be uncovered a century later (we were just 93 years early!) We kept that board as a memento, but it disappeared a few years later, perhaps taken by mistake to build one of our camps in the woods.

I like to say that the house I was born in was built just for me; it was completed in May 1942, just a few weeks before my arrival. After several renovations over the years, it is still our house today. And it stayed put for almost seven years until the day Mary was born, May 14, 1949, next door in Pépère's house. That's the day when Uncle Tony and his crew moved the house to another spot not far away, on the other side of the road.

Houses in Vacherie — and indeed all over southern Louisiana — were built on concrete pillars about 18 inches off the ground, to guard against the potential damage of floods. Some were higher, depending on the flood risk of the particular region. With the right equipment, houses could be moved from one place to another, across many miles if necessary. In fact, moving a whole house is still a common practice today.

Observing the moving of such a large edifice was an amazing feat for a young boy to witness. First, Uncle Tony spent several days jacking the house up on blocks and installing a double axel of wheels on the back underside. Then he hooked it up to a large truck, which pulled it ever so slowly a few hundred yards down the road, and deposited it on our new property — its present location. The move went so smoothly that a fish bowl on the kitchen table remained in place, no water spilled.

When that had been accomplished, we walked back to Pépère's house to welcome Mary into the world. She was just a few hours old, and I can still see my sister Lael taking Mary in her arms, and cuddling her on Mémère's rocker in the front room. I was afraid to touch her; she looked so tiny and fragile!

That was an exciting day for everyone, and marked a new phase in our lives.

Not long after the house was in place, work on remodelling began with the addition of two rooms to make space for future arrivals: Margaret in 1951 and Jude in 1953. A few decades later when Mama was working and my parents had the means to remodel, they reconfigured the house yet again into the more comfortable modern home it is today.

The older girls around the farm, Marjorie, Ina Claire, Kathleen...dressed my sister Lael and me as a bride and groom, 1945.
Note I am wearing Pépère's pants, goes around me twice, and his Panama.

The house in its new location, 1950, after the addition of two rooms, with its outbuildings. I'm standing in Aunt Adela's front yard.

Colin x 3

When my wife Hamida and I were traveling in Florida last January, we went to the small town of Madison to explore the history of my namesake, Capt. Colin P. Kelly, Jr. He was from that north Florida town, and there is a monument to his heroism that we wanted to see.

Let me explain... A few days after Pearl Harbor, on December 10, 1941, Captain Kelly was piloting a B-17 bomber out of Clark Field in the Philippines, attacking Japanese naval positions. He is remembered as the first American hero of the war after ordering his crew to bail out shortly before his bomber exploded, killing him. His was the first American B-17 to be shot down in combat.

In those dire times after Pearl Harbor, the country needed a hero to boost morale, and President Roosevelt saw to it that Captain Kelly got the full treatment. Later, Roosevelt wrote a letter to the future US president of 1956, who happened to be Dwight Eisenhower, asking him to bypass normal procedure to ensure Captain Kelly's son a place at West Point. When the young man came of age, however, he refused special treatment, applied to West Point himself, and was accepted on his own merits.

Referring to the elder Captain Kelly, the phrase, "Kelly, the hero" was often spoken in my family home, and my mother decided that if the baby she was expecting in June was a boy, she would name him Colin after that impressive man. And *voilà*, Colin P. Gravois.

When I was in the U.S. Army in Germany in the mid-1960s, I saw in the military newspaper, *The Stars and Stripes,* that Colin P. Kelly III (the hero's son) was also in the Army, and stationed in Frankfurt. He had graduated from West Point and was now a captain serving in the Chaplain Corps.

I made a note of that, and the next time I found myself in the Frankfurt area, I looked him up. The news article said he was stationed in the I.G. Farben Building, so I went up to that highly-guarded edifice and asked if it were possible to meet Captain Kelly — a sort of Colin-this-is-Colin meeting. When the M.P. at the entrance finally understood my "mission," he made an exception to the No Visitors policy, and a few minutes later Captain Kelly came down to meet with me. We exchanged pleasantries for a few minutes, and then wished each other good luck and parted.

My visit to his father's final resting place in Madison, Florida, closed the circle for me.

Madison, Florida, January 2020.

J. Victor Reulet
(1885-1952)

I can see from the many pictures of me in my little white playsuit that I spent a lot of time under the huge pecan trees over the course of my first three years nestled happily in the crook of my grandfather's arm. But my first vivid memory of Pépère Victor was formed on V-J Day, in September of 1945.

In memory's eye it is late afternoon, and everyone in my family is listening to the radio and talking at the same time. Of course, I didn't understand what was going on — only that the adults were all extremely pleased about something. There was great excitement all about. Everyone was hugging everyone else, hoisting the little ones in the air, then hugging everyone all over again.

There were a lot of "comings and goings" in the yard, too. At one point, Pépère drove up and parked his car under the trees as usual. Everyone ran out to meet him, excitedly.

My grandfather always commanded the center of attention, and I can still picture him that day in his favorite lounge chair under the pecan trees, surrounded by members of the family, offering his interpretation of the events of the day. I always remember him not only as a source of information but as a fount of wisdom for the rest of us.

Mama told me years later — and she was very fond of the story — that the only thing I was concerned about on V-J Day was getting a tricycle. We didn't actually know that fancy word; we called it simply, "a three-wheel bike." Because of the shortage of materials during the war, very few toys were produced, especially not things made of metal, and to my pleas that my parents get me a tricycle, the answer was always, "When the war is over." So, when I finally understood the reason why everyone was acting especially excited that day, I pulled Mama aside and pleaded, "Is Daddy going to bring my bike tonight?"

*

Our house was situated just south of the big pecan trees in the vast yard between Pépère's and Aunt Marie's, so as soon as I was able to run free, I spent a lot of time in both places. In summer, when Pépère returned from his daily rounds as a salesman (he sold farm products all over south Louisiana), he'd park his car under the trees to cool it off. Then he'd usually relax in the shade himself, with his newspapers and something cold to drink, like a big pitcher of iced lemonade. That was Pépère's idea of Heaven.

A few years before he died, he bought a free-standing hammock, and that became his favorite place to unwind — and also ours, four or five of us at a time, when he wasn't there. The hammock was sturdy and lasted well into the 1950s, at which point it finally just wore out. But to this day, seeing a hammock anywhere still gives me a warm feeling, because it reminds me of Pépère Victor.

*Another great afternoon under the pecan trees
in the crook of Pépère's arm.*

He was on the road a lot, and since he was a generous person, he often brought back treats for us...sweet cantaloupes, strawberries, jars of shucked oysters (which he loved fried), and many other things that roadside peddlers had for sale. I enjoyed waiting for him to come home because I knew there was usually a reward for me, like a big juicy orange or a slice of watermelon — another of Pépère's favorites.

One time, he brought back several cases of a red soda drink in big, quart-and-a-half sized bottles. I never knew what flavor it was exactly, but to us it was delicious, and we drank it all summer. So, it was either lemonade, ice cold water, soda, or some other drink, but Pépère always had to have something to cool down with after a long hot day on the road.

*

When I was around six or seven, I often helped Pépère with the cattle, mostly pumping water for the troughs on the hand-cranked pumps, or parceling out the feed. The feed sacks weighed about fifty pounds each and were made of a strong, brightly colored material; "prints," the ladies called them. If you did it right, once the sack was empty you could unravel the sewing at the seams by pulling on the right string, and then you'd end up with a large, square piece of cloth. We made many a dress, curtains, tablecloths, and other necessities out of those feed bags. But there was a small problem: you never knew what pattern or hue would show up on the next sack, and that made it difficult to color-coordinate your summer wardrobe!

One morning around 6 o'clock when I was seven years old, Pépère called to ask me to come see him. When I got to his house, he took me to the barn where Mémère was milking the cows and told me, "I think it's about time you took over Mémère's job, you're old enough now." He said he would pay me 50 cents a week, every Saturday. And if he ever forgot to pay me, I should just tell him, "My palm is itching." I kept that job long after he died, till I was about 16 years old, but the "salary" died with him after only two years on the job.

Sometimes the cattle would break away from the pastures, and we had to round them up. When that happened, Pépère would drive me out to the fields where the cows were roaming. Then he'd return to the house to wait while I drove them home. After that, we had to fix the hole in the fence that they had escaped through. Usually Boy Isom from across the road was around to give us a hand.

Pépère showing off his new horse, Snow. 1915, Vacherie.

At that time, there was no canal at the back end of his property; the present one was dug in 1954 for drainage. So, when it was dry in summer and the water had receded, we could drive a short distance into the woods in Pépère's car, then walk on ahead to look for stray cows. Along the way to the back, there was a spot where the dirt road slanted to the left and the car sort of careened for a few hundred feet before "righting" itself when the road leveled off. Now, in truth, all four wheels maintained contact with the ground so it was not really dangerous, but it *seemed* to be so to us young ones. That was always exciting, and every time we passed that slant in the road, Pépère accelerated a little and shouted, "Hold on, boys! Hold on! We're comin' through."

*

39

*Pépère, with guitar, serenading the arrival of his bosses'
new 1915 Model T Ford.*

Studio portrait, around 1905.

The roads in Vacherie were not blacktopped until 1949, and there was always the problem of loose gravel, the bane of travel then and one of my grandfather's pet peeves. He talked about that a lot since he spent most of his working hours on the road. And he also had to wrestle with flat tires, and pot-holes that "could swallow a car whole," he would say, and all the other vicissitudes of maintaining a vehicle.

Once when Pépère was driving my sister Lael and me to Uncle Philip's store in Front Vacherie, we hit a pile of loose gravel near the intersection of present-day La. 3127 and La. 20. The car fishtailed and then flipped over onto its right side. I remember someone pulling me out through the left rear window, which was-facing upward. None of us appeared to be injured, though, and some helpful passers-by managed to flip the car right-side up again. It turned out there was surprisingly little damage to it, so we continued driving on to the river. It was only when we arrived at Tante Elise's that she noticed Lael's back was bruised! We were transporting some big chains in the back seat — sugarcane bale, which is very heavy, and the grown-ups concluded that's what had injured her. They tucked Lael into bed to care of her, but I don't think a doctor ever came out to the house to examine her. Medical doctors lived too far away from us in those days, and Folk Medicine was still the trusted form of treatment.

For all his traveling, over all types of roads, under all kinds of conditions, Pépère had surprisingly few accidents. About the only other one I recall happened on a Saturday night on

Four Reulet daughters on a sunny April 1945 day: Bernice, Janice, Helen, Rosemary. Note the pecan trees are shorn of leaves yet.

41

the Bayou Chevreuil Road, near the little bridge on the Chackbay side. Pépère and Mémère, with Marjorie in tow, had taken Janice to the Saturday night dance at Mike's Place in Chackbay (where she would later meet Willie, her future husband). On the way back, near that bridge, a man named Plouke ran into them. Falgoust was his surname, I believe, but we knew him only by his nickname. Plouke was said to love a drink and may have been seeing double by that time of night. My grandfather's car was damaged beyond repair but only Mémère was injured — her back badly wrenched. It made a lasting impression on me to see her being brought home on a stretcher after her hospital visit. Or was it after a visit to Dr. Drake in Front Vacherie? I don't recall. But either way, it was scary seeing such a strong woman laid out on a stretcher. Before that, it had never occurred to me that either of grandparents could get sick or die.

Reulet family in wartime, 1942. Front, in uniform, a family friend René Steib; over his left shoulder Uncle Wood in uniform; behind Wood, Uncle John, who was soon to deploy in the Pacific.
Note: Fourth adult from the right, Aunt Rosemary, holding baby Colin (4 months).

Pépère liked the excitement of big outdoor gatherings and fairs, and when I was in the second grade, he took me to the South Louisiana State Fair in Donaldsonville, which was a big to-do back then. Mama pinned my name and address in my pants pocket in case I got lost, and away we went — Pépère, Mémère, Marjorie, Dick, and me.

That was a thrilling day! Traveling so far away from home; going on the rides; watching the sideshow barkers touting their charges: "Step right up and see the two-headed calf !"

"Come in! Come in! See the six-hundred-pound lady!"

"Over here, folks, for the man who eats scrap iron! Right this way!"

Pépère even let me go inside *The Maze* — a magical environment constructed of glass panels. I went through it with Dick and a few of the other grown-ups, and it felt just like being all grown up myself.

On the ride home, I had to sit on a sack of feed in the back seat, my head scraping the car's roof.

No idea how that feed bag got there because it sure wasn't there on the way over. Pépère Victor must have picked it up at the livestock exhibition.

*

One of the qualities that most impressed me about my grandfather was that he was an avid reader. He read *The Times-Picayune* daily, kept up to date on current events, and subscribed to several magazines including the *Literary Digest* and *Natural History,* which he loved.

(After his death, Mémère gave me the magazines until the subscriptions ran out.)

He loved to read and discuss books. As soon as he received a new one, he'd inscribe his name in flowing script on the inside front cover, and sometimes the back cover, including the date and time, to the exact minute. For example, he'd write:

J. Victor Reulet, Vacherie, Louisiana. Saturday, June 30, 1947. 3:51 p.m.

Sometimes he'd append a short message like the one below:

After his death, Pépère's library was dispersed among his children; over the years, they took what suited their fancy, and his grandson also took a few too, with Mémère's permission. It's easy to spot a book of his at someone's house because it's cloth-bound with no paper jacket, 1940's style, most often with a brown or gray spine. I invariably pick it up and look for the inscription. It's always a pleasure to see that beautiful handwriting again, and to read the notes he made in the margins. It makes me feel close to him, every time.

*

Pépère took a passionate interest in politics — local, state, national and with the war, international. He enjoyed discussing the issues of the day more than just about anything else in life. It was always lively around him. Sometimes in fact, the discussions got extremely heated, especially when he was debating an issue with a relative or close friend. But in time I came to understand that "heated" meant "with passion" and not "with ill feeling." Speaking with ill feeling would have been contrary to Pépère's very being. That said, the discussions did get hot, I can tell you, and he could turn alarmingly red in the face while driving his points home.

Pépère was a Huey Long man, through and through, a populist at heart, and he held several appointive and elective jobs himself over the years. Justice of the Peace, I believe, at one time. Deputy Sheriff (non-uniformed) at another. He even ran for the office of Police Juror (councilman) on the local governing body in 1936, some six months after Long's assassination. His campaign flyer for that election is a real keeper, ending with the line: "Give me a chance to dry somebody's tears."

Unfortunately, Pépère withdrew his candidacy some weeks before the election. The reason was that his daughter, Mae, was a school teacher in the parish and could have been fired if her father lost the election! Or even if he had won but was in the minority governing faction. This was before the advent of tenure for teachers. Anyway, that's the official family story of why Pépère dropped out, and we have no pre-election polls to determine what kind of horse race it would have been had he stayed in.

*

In today's parlance, Pépère Victor would be described as, "A people person" and, "An educated man." He was fully literate in both English and French, which was not usually the case with his contemporaries in our town. His early schooling was in Vacherie, then later he went to live for a few years with his Tante Dada (Aunt Amanda) in Franklin, where he also attended school for some time. But after four or five years of schooling it was time to start work — first on the farm, and then when he was 16,

Pépère Victor at a Woodmen convention in Shreveport, 1928.

for a man named Baudry who had a store in Front Vacherie by the river, near the present-day intersection of La. 18 & 20.

But when Pépère was around 20 years old, he realized that acquiring more education would help him get on in life, so he went to New Orleans where he attended Soulé College. While studying there, he worked at odd jobs to pay for his tuition, living expenses, and lodgings on Prytania Street.

One of his jobs was driving a streetcar for New Orleans Public Service. He would regale us with tales of those years, claiming he was the first person to drive a streetcar in McDonoughville, across the river from N.O., a community that has since become part of Harvey. He was also proud to say that he drove one of the first vehicles to cross the Huey P. Long Bridge the day it opened, and that his car was just behind the dignitaries! Wherever something interesting was happening in south Louisiana, Pépère Victor wanted to be part of it.

Living in New Orleans not only permitted him to further his education, but he often said it taught him many lessons that he used throughout his life. He was never in the least intimidated by city folk and was proud to retain "the country" in himself. But he was a good communicator, regardless of where someone came from. Richard Gravois, a New Orleans cousin, recalled an incident for me that illustrates Pépère's flexibility with people:

"His English and French were both very good because he dealt with so many people from all over. Once in New Orleans, when he was driving his city grandchildren around, he was stopped by a cop. I admit, I was surprised to hear him become inarticulate and stumble in broken Franglais about the situation. But the long and the short of it is: that cop did not write him a ticket."

Once, I took Aunt Mae and Mama on a little pilgrimage to see the house where Pépère lived in on Prytania Street, in the Lower Garden District. The sisters Reulet were thrilled. They inspected the house from the street, looking at it from all angles. It has been restored, but the little window on the third floor, through which Pépère surveyed the outside world from his room, is still there. After we examined the house, we walked around the neighborhood reminiscing about "Papa," as they called him. And later that day we had lunch at the restaurant "Victor" in the Ritz Carlton, in Papa Victor's honor.

Window, top floor right, from where Victor surveyed the world passing by on Prytania street while he attended Soulé College in New Orleans, 1905-1908.

Many friends and acquaintances around Vacherie came to my grandfather for help with various problems, usually on weekend mornings when they knew he'd be home. They often asked him to intercede with some government agency on their behalf; to write a formal letter, or fill out an official form; or even just to help solve a personal problem. They knew he was well-traveled and well-read, that he met people every day from all walks of life, and that few situations were foreign to him. They trusted him as a source of reliable counsel and were grateful for it. I remember those visits well and met many older Vacherie residents for the first time at Pépère's house, including Lazare Reulet, Terrence Oubre, and Benjamin Falgoust among many others.

Pépère had an easy manner, and his long years of traveling around the state polished his skills as a *raconteur*. Years after, when we'd meet someone who remembered him down Bayou Lafourche way, in Franklin, or in some other place, people were always happy to talk about him, recalling fondly how entertaining he was — always ready to share the latest story or amusing anecdote. Everyone agreed: Pépère Victor was an exceptionally good story-teller.

Of the thousands of memories I have of my grandfather, the most vivid is from the day he died.

It was a Friday evening in January, 1952. I had spent time with him that afternoon after school, doing odd jobs in the yard, and had just returned home. It was around 5:30 p.m. and we were eating supper — grilled meat with butter beans and rice — a menu etched on my memory forever. While we were at the table, Tante Yette (Daddy's sister, Henrietta, from down the road) called to talk to Mama. At that time, all the telephones in Vacherie were on party lines, and if the line was occupied you had to wait until the conversation was over before you could make your call. The only exception was an emergency; if something was truly urgent, you could butt in and ask for the line.

Tante Yette's and Pépère's phones were on the same eight-party line. Suddenly, someone broke in and cried, "Emergency! Emergency! I need the line!" Mama hung up, startled, and said some lady had asked them to get off the line, and it sounded serious. A few seconds later, just the time it took to dial our number (4333), the phone rang. It was Mama's youngest sister, Marjorie. She was calling to tell us to rush over; Pépère had fallen in the kitchen, hit his head, and was unconscious!

We took off running. Uncle Lewis, who was home on leave from the Air Force, had already run over to get Aunt Marie from next door. When we got there, Pépère was lying on the floor with Marie cradling his head and saying prayers. I remember his face had a bluish color to it. The house was in a state of bedlam.

A short time later it was determined that Pépère had passed from this world.

A hush fell over the house as the sense of desperate urgency to get care for him gradually gave way to a calm acceptance of his passing.

Then things happened fast. Mémère happened to be in Thibodaux attending a religious event at Stark Field, the baseball park. A discussion ensued about how to get in touch with her there. A few years ago, when J.B. Falgoust was at our house in Paris, we were talking about Pépère, and he said he had gone to that event with Paul Delattre and Mémère had ridden with them. Anyhow, contacting her got taken care of some kind of way, and soon Mémère was en route back to Vacherie.

But then there was the problem of calling family members who were living farther away. I know they got hold of Uncle Raymond and the other boys in Baton Rouge fairly easily, but the problem remained of how to alert Aunt Mae in New Orleans and Aunt Bernice, who was living in Greenville, Mississippi, at the time. We needed to get Uncle Gaston and Uncle

Woodie on the phone as soon as possible, so they could gently break the news to Mae and Bernice.

Then there was the problem of Janice. She worked in New Orleans and returned to Vacherie every Friday evening around seven p.m. on Ben Rome's bus. Someone would have to be at the road to meet her and inform her of Pépère's death before she came into the house, to cushion the shock.

People soon started pouring in from Baton Rouge and other places and there was talk of trying to get the coroner, Dr. Nobile, to come. That was especially important because when Pépère fell, he hit the front of the stove, and there was a mean gash on his head. Ruling his death "an accident" instead of "from natural causes" could have made a difference in an insurance settlement. But in the end, the coroner did not make the trip to Vacherie. He ruled it "a natural death" from his office in Convent — and that was that. Back then, people were far more inclined to accept those kinds of events than they would be today.

After the coroner issue was settled, the grown-ups started to make arrangements with the funeral home, but I don't know what happened after that. Sometime around 10 p.m., my sister, Lael, and I were taken next door to Tante Adela's house (Ina Claire's house today) to spend the night. We slept in their living room with me on the sofa.

Pépère's wake was held in the house, as was the custom in Vacherie in those days, with the body in an open casket in the living room. His funeral took place on Sunday afternoon at 3 o'clock.

The lives of all he touched changed dramatically; everyone took the loss very hard. I was still a boy, and this was the first time anyone central to my life had died. It was the first time I felt the reality of the old cliché: "There was a big empty place against the sky."

*

A few days after the funeral, I was over at Mémère's house watching Uncle Earl go through Pépère's papers, with my little sister Mary, who was about two-and-a-half at the time, playing in the room. Uncle Earl had just found Pépère's pistol in the desk. (Pépère usually kept it in one of the pigeon hole drawers at the top.) The kids in our family liked to say that Pépère Victor slept with his pistol under his pillow and would put it back in the desk every morning when he got up. But that was probably just starry-eyed speculation on the part of his impressionable grandchildren.

Anyway, Uncle Earl sat down on Pépère's bed in the closed-in side porch to take a closer look at the pistol. It was a large, black gun, and he turned it over and over in his hands, commenting on its size and weight. Mary and I were standing on either side of him, watching closely. The sight of that pistol — and Uncle Earl handling it — had raised the level of tension in the room considerably.

At a given moment, Earl had the pistol in his lap, and while manipulating it, he absentmindedly actioned the magazine. The gun went off with a thunderous roar. I still remember the bitter stench of gunpowder. Thankfully, the bullet passed between us, but it came perilously close to hitting little Mary — less than a foot from her head! It smashed through the window and then through the metal reflector on the outside lights. We were all shocked, but Uncle Earl was the most shaken of all when he realized how close he had brought us to a catastrophe.

The damaged reflector stayed up for a good many years after that, and we frequently pointed to the bullet hole to impress visitors, like our city cousins.

*

Sometimes when I'm at home in Vacherie, where Pépère's desk sits today, and have a moment alone, I quietly open the desk, lower the front panel, look into a few little drawers, and dream of the time when the desk sat in its comfortable corner by the window in my grandfather's room. Silent friend to a highly expressive man. A charismatic man with a broad reach. Beloved by many.

WHAT IF?

Over the years I have often thought: *What if?* What if Pé-père Victor had lived 10 or 15 years longer? Ten more years would have taken him to 76, not an old age at all (I'm 78). Think of all the active people we know today who are around that age. Five of his daughters lived into their nineties and were still remarkably alert and active, so it seems likely, had Pépère not had that fatal heart attack in 1952 he could have been around with us a lot longer.

He would have seen the extraordinary changes of the 1950s and '60s, which I am sure he would have loved being a part of: The Interstate Highway system, constructed, of course, *specially* for him, a traveling salesman; Medicare; the civil rights struggle; women's liberation; the Kennedy assassination (the defining moment of our generation.) And he would have taken an immense pleasure in seeing his grandchildren grow up and start lives of their own. He would have loved to part of all that.

And for me, looking back, I think of all those stories not told, those roads not taken, those meals not eaten, those friends not met, those joys not shared. Spending another ten or fifteen years with him around would have enriched my life immeasurably.

But then again, my life was already so vastly enriched because of him being there for me those first nine years.

Studio photo Pépère Victor,
New Orleans 1920, he was 25.

THE DUPONTS MOVE IN

One Saturday, not long after our house was moved to its new place, two flatbed trucks bearing a mixed confusion of household furniture and supplies pulled into the yard of the old house across the road. It was the Dupont family arriving in force: Joseph, Josephine, and an assortment of little Duponts — among them, Eddie, who was to become my great friend and faithful hunting companion for the next five years.

Eddie was a year older than me, and at that age a one-year difference is important. He was stronger, taller, more streetwise — and most especially, a lot more "woods wise" than me. I don't remember where the Duponts lived before moving to our neighborhood, but they appeared to feel like they had gone upscale coming there.

The Duponts lived somewhat on the margins of society, and although Joseph worked steadily, he was very partial to Regal beer, which no doubt contributed to the fact that they were still reduced to renting, even at his advanced stage of life. Their rental was an old rundown pile of a house, with "full outdoor plumbing."

Now, in truth, the Duponts were not what Mama considered the best company to keep. But I guess she didn't feel Eddie was *too* bad of an influence on me, because she let me run around with him in the fields and woods, and although she drew the line at having the whole family over at our house, with their innumerable children, she didn't mind letting Eddie come and go as he pleased.

"Eddie is a nice, quiet boy," she said approvingly.

Joseph and Josephine did not speak English very well, and of course that limitation was passed down to the little Duponts. I always got a kick out of it when Eddie would say, "Tomorrow is my daddy's per day," (meaning *pay* day). Or when he said happily, "Tonight, Daddy's gonna bring us some Hershey balls!" (Hershey *bars*.)

With anticipation brimming over, he made that announcement every other Friday (his dad's *per day*). I guess when you're a family with little extra money to spend on the kids,

First day of school, September 1952.
From left: Eddie, me, the Rougee brothers, Ralph,
Raymond, and Alfred, and my sister, Lael.

"Hershey balls" make a very special treat. To this day, I think of Eddie warmly whenever I spot Hershey bars in a candy rack at the gas station or when I see one of those shops specializing in pay day loans.

The Duponts always seemed to be "a few cents short of a dollar." Josephine blamed her financial woes on Joseph. She grumbled that he doled out money in nickels and dimes, and even that pittance only when he was in a generous mood. When Josephine was in a "difficult situation," she'd send one of the little girls around to a neighbor to plead poverty in her best local French:

"Mom po-lay cassé so billet de 20 piastres, li demande si t'as pas 15 sous pour ajette nous du lait."

(Mama doesn't want to break her twenty-dollar bill. She'd like to borrow 15 cents to buy some milk for us.)

Mrs. Dupont appeared to have an endless supply of big bills that she didn't want to break. Sometimes, in fact, she didn't even want to break a one-dollar bill! Her financial savvy dictated that she didn't ask the same neighbor twice in a row, but rotated among five or six "creditor moms" in the neighborhood, and when, a week or two later, the borrowing circuit had been completed, she started the rounds all over again.

Her favorite *soft touch* was my kind-hearted aunt, Tante Adela, who lived right next door to her. One story, which we called The Coconut Story, made us laugh every time Aunt Marie told it. She was very fond of repeating it, too, and it got better and better, because with each telling, she had an opportunity to polish her imitation of Josephine's "not-so-standard" French, physical mannerisms, and tone of voice.

One morning, Josephine crossed over to Tante Adela's and sheepishly told her it was Joseph's birthday and she would like to surprise him with a cake that night — but she was a tad short of some basic ingredients. Could Adela "advance" her a little flour, sugar, and a few other things — just until next week?

Tante Adela could be sentimental and had a soft spot for requests of that nature, especially from people she knew to be poor, so she parceled out generous portions of sugar and flour and even threw in six eggs and a lump of yeast, saying:

"You tell Joseph Happy Birthday from us."

Josephine thanked her profusely, then started on her way back home. But after only a few steps, she stopped, turned around, and said pleadingly, "You know, Adela, Joseph just *loves* coconut cake. You wouldn't happen to have a little coconut handy, would you?"

*

The Duponts moved to Front Vacherie some years later when Joseph's employers found them an old house near the machine shop where he worked. Eddie, of course, moved with them, and for a while I was left to go tramping around the fields and woods alone — at least until I fell in with a few other boys. But no one could replace Eddie. He was my best running-around pal — and that was that.

We were reunited the following summer when I went to spend a day with him at his family's house. As Daddy dropped me off that morning (his workplace was only a few hundred feet down the street from the Dupont home) he admonished me, "Now, Colin, I don't want to see you running all around the neighborhood all day, you hear?"

Eddie had other plans for us — we would explore the area in back of the Mississippi River levee, a place I had never been before. He also promised we'd go skinny dipping in the Mississippi — another first for me. All of this was far more to my liking than hanging around their small yard all day. However, we had one obstacle ahead of us: how to get past Daddy's place of business without him seeing us, since the sidewalk that led to the Mississippi passed right in front of his shop.

After playing out different scenarios, the plan we finally settled on was that I would walk on Eddie's left, sticking to him and keeping in step with him as best I could. (He was taller than me, remember, so naturally his stride was longer.) If my father saw us, we would say Eddie's mother had sent us on an errand to the Hubble store to buy some rice.

We practiced a bit before taking off, and by the time we arrived at Daddy's shop we had the routine down pat. But when we were just past the gas pumps and it looked like clear sailing, a friendly voice rang out loudly:

"Colin! What you doing here?" and, "Hé, Paul, ga ça qui la!" ("Hey, Paul, look who's here!")

It was Leelique (Alexander Mitchell), an employee who was pumping gas out front. He sounded delighted to see me. (One rule of survival in the White world was: *Always be friendly to the boss's son.*) And I would have been very happy to run into him, too — had it been at another time and place.

Leelique (pronounced, "Lee-leek") was a wonderful man, loved by all, and in the small world of Vacherie humorists, he was credited with an immortal line concerning Dr. Charles Daunus, a physician who had set up a medical practice in Vacherie some years before.

My father's place of work, he's in the middle next to his sister. Far right: Leelique. Down the street on the left is the levee we scampered over.

Dr. Daunus was lightyears ahead of his time in his respect for African Americans. For starters, he had only one, multiracial waiting room. Secondly, he had no "separate but equal" bathroom facilities. Often in the 1950s, you would see signs in public establishments on the doors of three separate bathrooms: MEN, WOMEN, and COLORED, and to have integrated waiting rooms or bathrooms was a huge *No-No* in the American south at the time.

Now, perhaps running a racially integrated clinic had its economic advantages — savings on redundancy, among other things, but Daunus made no apologies to anyone and just plowed on ahead. After a while, people stopped talking about it, and it became a non-issue. Daunus was a no-nonsense kind of a person, and that policy seemed to serve him just fine.

He also had a well-deserved reputation for being "quick on the draw," meaning: swift and effective with his scalpel. He performed scores of surgeries alone or with the help of one assistant who was not necessarily an RN. But he prided himself in never having lost a patient on the operating table. (Can't fault him there.)

Now, back to the story about Leelique's remark...

Dr. Daunus had operated on Leelique for appendicitis, and for the years following, whenever the conversation got around to the doctor, Leelique would say, in his most colorful Creole, eyes gleaming:

"Daunus, huh! L'apé filé son couteau même avant toe traverse track la!"

("Daunus, huh! He's starts sharpening his knife (scalpel) even before you cross the tracks!")

(We had to drive over the railway tracks to get to Dr. Daunus's from Back Vacherie.)

Now, for people who don't speak Creole, I can see where the English translation might not be funny. But in the original, it broke us up, just broke us up every time. It was all in his delivery. Leelique was droll; he was entertaining; he was a round ball of merriment. All you had to do was look at him and you'd start laughing with pure delight.

Yes, indeed. Leelique was the kind of man you can think back on, even 30 years after he's gone to his grave, and you still feel like laughing. Miss him to this day.

Thanks to Leelique's "enthusiastic" welcome, Daddy came out to the front of the shop, listened to our story about buying Josephine's rice, and said, "Huh. Well, Okay, now, but you boys better get that rice and come right back."

We took off running! But when we reached the corner of La. 20, in front of Beck's Garage, after a precautionary glance behind us, we scampered up and over the levee in three seconds flat. We were *safe* for the time being! Oh, sure, we knew we would have to devise another plan to get by the shop on the way back. But since that was hours in the future (which for youngsters feels like a long time), for now at least, we were in Boy Heaven.

The no man's land behind the levee the locals called *batture*, from Canadian French. Eddie knew the area well, where the fishing ponds were, and where we could catch some baby turtles. We captured about a dozen that day, and I sold them the next day for 10 cents each to Harry Perque, a man who had a business supplying small turtles to people who fancied such things in New Orleans. He also bought grasshoppers and small lizards which he sold to research laboratories. Some people can find a way to make a living anywhere with anything, it seems!

So, there we were, a local version of Tom and Huck, frolicking around the Mississippi.

I had read *Tom Sawyer* and *Huckleberry Finn* that school year, and I entertained Eddie with some of their exploits. We even made big plans to float down the Mississippi together later, when we were in high school.

The best thing about that day's adventures was skinny dipping in the river. My first impression was that it was deadly cold. With 100-degree weather outside, it was a shock to go into the water and find it almost freezing. But as the water comes down from as far north as Minnesota, it does make sense.

The current was strong so we hugged the shore, taking no chances. We swam and splashed around. We mooned some boats and barges! A few people on one barge even mooned us back!

To return home, we had to avoid passing in front of Daddy's workplace at this late hour. We ended up walking behind the levee a quarter mile to a big sugarhouse, where we quickly crossed back over, and made our way to Eddie's house through the cane fields without a hitch.

It had been a fun day, reuniting with Eddie and swimming in the Mississippi, but it was fast approaching five o'clock, and I had to go meet Daddy at the shop to return home with him.

*

The next time I saw Eddie was in high school. He had been held back, and I caught up with him in the 9th grade. But our duo never got together again. Things change, and even the best of pals can drift apart. Sometimes quietly. Without a word said about it. One boy naturally moves upriver. And the other drifts...downward.

What's In A Picture?

This slightly blurry photo of me at the age of one, in July, 1943, was taken under the pecan trees, our favorite place. I'm waving a stick at the camerawoman — my mother — amusing my older sister Lael. The photo is posted here to illustrate several characteristics of farm life in Vacherie at the time.

Aunt Marie's House. In the background, we see Aunt Marie Reulet's house (Cousin Dick's now), built in 1921 by Uncles Jean and Tétin. First, they purchased and dismantled a two-story boardinghouse in Front Vacherie that had been home to the workers before the lumber camps left town. Then they used the wood to reconstruct a building in a configuration typical of farm houses in our area. Note that the house is not painted; most were not in those days.

Barrière a pieux. Starting from the left side of the picture is the picket fence made from cypress wood, a *barrière a pieux.* Cypress is rot proof, and consequently most people used it for that type of fence, especially since cypress was still plentiful in those days.

Cistern. Next you can see the round cypress cistern that collected water from the roof for drinking and cooking.

Caillette. At the foot of the steps, we see Aunt Marie's cow Caillette, resting in the shade. That was a very common name for a cow then; almost everyone had a Caillette. We lost her a few years later when she got stuck in the mud crossing a ditch in the pasture behind the house, and we had to call Boy to try to extricate her. Sadly, he was unsuccessful, and eventually he had to put her out of her misery.

Petit garde manger. In every kitchen there was a *garde manger* — a large cupboard for keeping food and dishes. There was also a *petit garde manger* for keeping milk, butter, and other perishables overnight; this was before electricity and fridges came to Vacherie. The *petit garde manger* was always situated on a porch high up near the ceiling, where the (hopefully) cool breezes could keep things from "turning" on a hot summer night. In the picture, you can see the "box" on the back porch at the top of the steps, up on the wall between the two doors, it was screened on three sides.

Little wagon. Left over from farm days (1920's and 30's), we took a lot of rides around the yard in that wagon, mostly with a bigger person or two pulling us.

Shutters. These handmade, wooden shutters were called *persiennes*, as they were "articulated" and could be opened or closed like blinds. If you look closely you will notice a wooden rod running down the middle of each shutter, connected to each "leaf" (blind), so you could open or shut the blinds easily with one hand. They were constructed in two sections, lower and upper. Some individual blinds fell off after years of usage, and the shutters eventually became nonfunctioning and had to be taken down by the mid-fifties.

The picket fence under the house. Once when I was three years old, Aunt Marie gave me a small hammer as a present. "Learn how to build something," she said. Well, I made a beeline to her house, crawled underneath through a hole in the pickets, and found myself in the area where they kept foodstuffs, potatoes, onions, etc., and wine in ten-gallon glass *donjons* ("dome-jones," we called them). The containers had a wicker-like protective sheath, and the family legend is that I selected a few where the wicker was partially missing, and gave them a few good whacks just for fun — and there went next year's wine.

Front porch. To the extreme right of the photo, you can see a glimpse of the large front porch with its several inviting rocking chairs, where we spent many an evening.

The shade. We grew up under the pecan trees, and you see here a small portion of the total shaded area they provided. It was an immense playground, and we never tired of the cool summer breezes and the shade of our beloved trees, where we made ice cream in Aunt Marie's hand-cranked freezer in summer.

Vacherie, A Brief History

In 1716, a Scottish financier named John Law founded the *Banque Générale* in Paris. It was a private bank which had the authority to print money. Law was a dreamer and a schemer. He persuaded the French government to combine his bank with the Mississippi Company (known as Company of the Indies), which had been set up by royal fiat to colonize the lower Mississippi Valley.

John Law in all his finery, 1715.

Law rapidly became closely involved with the French government and was appointed *Contrôleur Général des Finances*. His role was to raise capital, but his methods were not always above aboard. The shady manner in which he promoted his company led to massive speculation, and stock prices ballooned to over 60 times their original value! The word "millionaire" was coined at that time.

To develop the colony of Louisiana it was vital to attract settlers. The company put out advertisements far and wide to entice people to volunteer. The promotional literature described Louisiana as "A land filled with gold, silver, copper, and lead mines!" The vast majority of applicants were German-speaking people from Alsace, Germany, and Switzerland.

When the *émigrés* arrived in New Orleans in the 1720s, the city could not absorb such a large increase in population, so they gave the newcomers a Land Grant 25 miles upriver in the area of present-day St. Charles Parish. The region is referred to as The German Coast.

The new arrivals, expecting to find easy fortune, felt completely betrayed when they landed in an uncleared swampland of alligators and mosquitoes. Duped by John Law's deceitful publicity, they were now marooned in the wilderness with no way to return. Their only solution was to make it work or perish — so they made it work.

These immigrants were of hardy stock which stood them well, because they had to clear sizeable pieces of land to establish settlements. The upside was that their domain quickly became an important source of produce for New Orleans.

As the German Coast established itself into a sustainable permanent settlement, some robust souls eventually pushed across Lac Des Allemands ("Lake of the Germans"), situated to the rear of the settlement, to encamp on the western shores where Vacherie was founded in the 1780s by Antoine Foltz, a third-generation settler. (The name was later "French-i-fied" to Folse.) Once enough land had been cleared for pastures, the settlement became an important source of meat. Folse set up a *vacherie* (the French term for a cattle producing area) to raise livestock for the New Orleans market.

And that is the origin of the name of our town: Vacherie.

Antoine Folse may be given credit for founding Vacherie, but many pioneers, both German and French were instrumental in developing the region in the early years. Later in the 1800s immigrants like Graugnards, Reynauds, Caires, Bordelons and many others arrived directly from France and brought their own *savoir-faire* to the area. It is that mix of German, Spanish, French, Acadian, African, and Native American that gives our part of the U.S. its inimitable character and flavor.

*

In 1763, France ceded the colony of Louisiana to Spain following the French and Indian War. The Spanish language then took precedence over French on official documents, but the people continued to speak French. Spain held on to Louisiana until 1803, when the territory became a part of the United States after the Louisiana Purchase.

During the 1760s and 70s, another group of *émigrés* settled in Louisiana. These were the French-speaking Acadians from New Brunswick and Nova Scotia in Canada, who were expelled when that territory was ceded to the English after the French lost the French and Indian War. It was a story similar to what had occurred for the Germans 40 years previously: New Orleans could not absorb such a large number of new arrivals at one time. Instead, they were given a Land Grant 25 miles upriver from the German Coast (and 50 miles from New Orleans), on what became known as The Acadian Coast (*La Cote des Acadiens*), an area just a few miles from present-day Vacherie.

And in due course, the original German settlement of Vacherie was overtaken by French-speaking Acadians. Ultimately the French culture won out, and many German names were changed to French when francophone priests wrote out baptismal certificates. Zweig (which means twig) became La Branche; Himmel (sky) became Hymel; Huber became Oubre; Dubs...Toups; Rummel...Rome; Foltz...Folse.

*

When Napoleon sold Louisiana to the United States in 1803 (it had been Spanish for 40 years at that point) French again became the official language, and what was left of the German language and ethos was subsumed into the ascending French culture. And by the middle of the 19th century, English came into common use as a second language, since Louisiana was now part of the American union. However, starting around 1900, English began taking precedence over French when the teaching of French in schools as the primary language ended, and that foreshadowed the gradual encroachment of English into the lives of the French-speaking populace.

Up to WWII Louisiana French was the lingua franca of the state below the Red River, the traditional dividing line between North and South Louisiana. The use of French varied, family to family. My Gravois grandparents, who lived into the 1950s, did not speak a word of English, for example, while my Reulet grandparents were fully bilingual. My parents were also fully bilingual, but they decided for school purposes to make our home English speaking. (Children who started first grade with no English had a difficult time adapting.)

*

The southern part of Louisiana — the Greater Mississippi Delta — which Vacherie finds itself in the very center of, was created by land built up over millenia by annual spring flooding. Thousands of years ago, the present geographical location of Vacherie was in the warm waters of the Gulf of Mexico; now it's about 40 miles from the sea.

Until the 1940s, the rate of growth of the Louisiana coastline was about one mile every 16 years. But after WWII rampant oil exploration resulted in the building of canals in the marshes and lowlands, changing the flow of sediment-carrying waters in many places. Factor in the rising seas due to climate change, and we now see a disappearing coast. One statistic has it that Louisiana is losing approximately 25 to 35 square miles of land per year — or one football field every 15 minutes! More than 2,500 square miles have washed away in the past 75 years. At the current rate, if nothing is done to reverse the trend (and erosion rates are growing exponentially), by 2050 an estimated 750,000 acres (which is an area the size of Rhode Island) will disappear. Vacherie may well end up in the middle of the Gulf waters again.

*

The alluvial soil on both sides of the Mississippi was extremely fertile and became valuable farmland, and the growing of indigo, and later rice and sugarcane, hastened its development. Investors from New York and other financial centers sank fortunes into the region, and that influx of capital underwrote the rise of the great plantations. By 1860, the stretch of land on both sides of the Mississippi between New Orleans and Baton Rouge was one of the most affluent parts of the country. It was claimed that there were more millionaires in that part of Louisiana than in the whole of the Northeast.

Of course, that enormous wealth was piled up on the backs of African slaves, and the end of the Civil War brought that economy built on free labor to a crashing halt. But by 1900, in spite of financial panics and numerous bankruptcies (most plantations changed hands several times), the economy had rebounded to some semblance of its former strength — but this time worked by paid labor.

*

Vacherie was founded just a few years after the arrival of the Acadians. As further land was cleared, more plantations were created, and the area flourished. Roads were built to connect the small communities along the River. The developed lands fronting the Mississippi, where the Acadians had landed, stretched for 40 miles downriver to the original German settlements. In the middle of all that, on the West Bank of the Mississippi, was Vacherie.

After a number of years two distinct Vacherie communities arose: one along the Mississippi (the "front" in local parlance) and one near the original Vacherie (the "back"), toward the lake and swamps, separated by five miles of sugarcane fields. Eventually the names of Front Vacherie and Back Vacherie came into common usage. Of course, originally, these two areas were called *Devant la Vacherie* and *Derrière la Vacherie.*

Until the middle of the 20th century, the Black community consisted chiefly of field workers, and they lived largely in plantation quarters. Very few owned their house. Compared to cotton farming where Black sharecropping was a way of life, there were only a small number of African American "croppers" in sugarcane farming. Unlike cotton, raising cane demanded intense cultivation, and the overhead was costly. It was just too difficult to make a living in sugarcane with a small plot of land.

Workers who toiled on huge farms had an open tab at the plantation store for buying the essentials. They subsisted on credit all year, and during the sugarcane harvest ("the grinding season") they earned enough money to clear their bill. Then they started all over again with a new line of credit to be cleared at the end of that year. They were essentially tied to the plantation and "owed their soul to the company store," as the song went.

It was not until after WWII with the advent of mechanization on farms, and when shipyards and manufacturing concerns opened in the New Orleans area, that Blacks were able to break away from plantation peonage and start earning real money. Then beginning in the 1950s refineries and industrial plants were constructed along the Mississippi River which opened new job opportunities. But, of course, it took the Civil Rights Acts of the mid-1960s to level the playing field as far as non-discriminatory hiring practices were concerned. And then, too, many Blacks were part of the Great Migration to the northern states and to California. Today very few remain in the quarters on plantations or do fieldwork. Mexicans on temporary work visas have taken their place.

BLACK STORIES

(Part I)

DR. LESLIE THEARD, SR., PHD

Les Theard was born in New Orleans in 1934. He graduated from Xavier University in the city, and he and his twin brother, Lowell, attended Notre Dame in South Bend, Indiana, where they completed a PhD program in Chemistry. In his mid-thirties, around the time his brother decided to become a medical doctor, Les earned an MBA from the University of Houston and Harvard Business School. Since his retirement in 1999, he spends the autumn and winter months in New Orleans and the spring and summer in Paris.

Les's first recollection of becoming aware that race is a highly charged issue was when he was about three years old. His family was in an unusual situation for Blacks in New Orleans, because they lived on the grounds of one of the most elegant homes in the entire state of Louisiana — the Robinson Mansion — located in the Garden District.

Les's father, Malgy, took a job which required him to live on the premises (albeit in the servants' quarters). The mansion was vacant, and the owners were concerned about keeping it safe and in good shape. Malgy's only duty was to make the rounds of the property when he was home in the evening. His compensation included living quarters on the property for himself and his family. That's how the Theards found themselves living in an exclusive, White section of town — the circumstance that led to Les's first encounter with the race issue.

Les's mother, Lavina, took her three young sons out every day for walks around the neighborhood. But on one particular afternoon, four-year-old Sonny commented on a young White girl who lived across the street (her name was Precious). Lavina realized that he had a blossoming interest in her. Of course, it was just a playful interest because the child was four — not fourteen. But he had apparently been talking to the girl, and their budding friendship set Lavina on edge. She stopped her three boys dead in their tracks and admonished Sonny harshly, "You can't do this, Sonny! You have to stop talking to her right now, and that's that!"

Les was listening but didn't really understand. Remember, he was only three. But things became clearer when his mother explained the situation to Sonny, "You're a *Negro*. She's *White*. We do not interact with White people! Period." Les remembers his mother's voice sounding stern, "I don't ever want to hear of you speaking to that young girl again! That's *out*."

A few years later they moved to another section of town around the time the boys started school. Les's parents were keenly aware of the difference in the educational quality between the two local schools for Blacks — a public school and a parochial school. Now, the public school, Thomy Lafon, was located one block from where they lived, while Holy Ghost School was about a seven-block walk. The boys would have loved to go to Thomy Lafon with their pals, but Lavina and Malgy were clear: The quality of education a child got at Holy Ghost was far superior to what they would get in the public school.

Les Theard, standing, and his twin brother Lowell.
New Orleans 2018.

So, Thomy Lafon was out of the question, even though Holy Ghost wasn't free like the public school. There was a modest charge, not enormous by middle class standards, but Les's father was basically a laborer, so paying that tuition was a challenge for him. Malgy and Lavina considered their children's education of the upmost importance — that's what they both worked so hard to provide. And Malgy always shouldered more than one job at a time — at least two — sometimes even three — to ensure the children's future.

*

Les recalls how the question of race was handled by the nuns in his school: "I didn't learn that it was a negative thing to be Black; that was not pumped into me. The nuns' strategy was to ignore race completely, and to treat us the way, I surmise, they were treated."

The nuns in Les's school were White; the priests were White; the police were White; even the garbage men were White, because garbage collecting was considered a privileged job in those days; the mail carriers were White; the bus drivers were White; the doctors and lawyers and judges were White. Virtually all positions of authority, responsibility and status were held by White people — and this was taken for granted in the White community. Blacks only held menial jobs; they were not permitted to come inside the great houses except as domestics; they had few resources available for education and activities; they were relegated to the back of the church and the back of the bus — and on and on. This was "normal." This was segregation.

*

When Les was older, he realized that segregated seating on a bus was a blunt statement: *Blacks are inferior*. One incident that brought home the fundamental fiction of the *separate but equal* concept happened on a Greyhound bus ride from Notre Dame to New Orleans. Since Les is *"of light skin"* (to use the popular phrase of the time), sometimes people thought he was Middle Eastern or Italian. This is apparently what happened on that bus ride.

Leaving Chicago, people were seated all over the bus, but when they pulled into Yazoo City, Mississippi, two burly White policemen got on and walked up and down the aisle, pointing at Blacks, "You! YOU! GET! Get back. You, too. Get on to the back."

Les was seated in the front but the cops passed him by. Although they looked at him, they must have assumed he was something other than Black.

After the two cops had "straightened it all up," one told the other, "Okay, all's in order now. Let's go." But as the second officer arrived at the front of the bus to disembark, he took a closer look at Les, and yelled in his face, "Say, YOU. Get your black ass on back there."

*

Les has a particular gripe against people (like a woman he met with the NAACP Speakers Bureau) who suggest he had nothing to be unhappy about because he was well educated and had achieved a lot in life. Regardless of his accomplishments, Les told me it was so deeply inculcated in him that Whites are superior, to the point where, "When I so much as spoke to a White person, I started shuddering in my boots!" That truly saddens him. He says White peoples' methods to intimidate Blacks were very effective. The message was: "You people are inferior, and if I show any kindness to you, you should feel fortunate. I'm a really good person; I bestow dignity on you by deigning to speak to you."

*

Les's father was from the Vacherie area, Moonshine quarters, and his mother was a native of Montz, a small settlement on the Mississippi outside of New Orleans. They met in the city where both had come to find work. So, it's just an accident of history that Les was born there; he could very well have been a country boy, and who knows what would have become of his life had he spent his formative years in the plantation setting of Moonshine. Something to contemplate.

*

Les has one more thing to say about race and how segregation affected him at Notre Dame. Although he had gained a lot of confidence in his abilities in parochial school and at Xavier University, where his self-esteem was reinforced by first-rate nuns and teachers, he says he was apprehensive about whether he could make it in the White world: "At age 22, when I started graduate school at Notre Dame, my confidence was shaky. Yeah, they told me I had a great education, and it probably was, but I still wondered: *Will I be able to cut it in the wider world?* That's pathetic."

"After 22 years and all that fine education, I still had a lot of self-doubt. The inferiority attitude had been so firmly ingrained in me; I hadn't gotten rid of it. And, you know something, I wonder if I'll *ever* get rid of it."

CAPT. GARFIELD KELLER

Garfield's story is particularly poignant. As a Black child born on a sugar plantation, he had little schooling, got married at 20, and joined the Army. While in the service, he received a high-school equivalency diploma (GED). After the Army, he went back to his hometown and worked at odd jobs. Eventually he was hired as a deputy sheriff with the responsibility of policing Black neighborhoods. Then, from being a token Black deputy, he worked his way up to the rank of Chief Deputy. In that role, he was boss of every deputy in the department — Black and White.

I can't help thinking of what this man might have accomplished in life had he had the same opportunities as Whites. Obviously, he demonstrated special gifts by rising as high as he did when coming from such grim circumstances. Moreover, he didn't express resentment about those conditions in all the time I knew him. That was one extraordinary quality of his character. He seemed to be able to face the injustices of segregation with a complete lack of bitterness — a kind of largesse and even wisdom — that made him a man of remarkable personal power.

*

Garfield Keller was born in 1934 into a family of ten children on Golden Star Plantation in Vacherie. His family lived in a cottage in the field workers' quarters — not a shotgun dwelling, but not fancy either. (A "shotgun house," by the way, is a structure, "...where you can shoot a gun from the front door and the bullet will go all through the house without hitting a wall.") Garfield's family house had a tin roof and was of the single-wall construction variety where the exterior wall is also the interior wall. There was no insulation, and some rooms didn't even have a ceiling! But it was considered comfortable, compared with other workers' houses. "We always felt we lived in style," Garfield told me, "because we didn't know anything better."

Garfield's father was a plowman, behind a mule, and he happened to be exceptionally good at it. Later, he became the caretaker of the mule barn. That was a promotion, which is why Garfield's family lived in slightly better quarters than the regular field workers. As manager of the mule barn, Mr. Keller was put on "running time," so rather than being paid by the hour, he was paid by the day. Most plantation workers were paid by the hour or even by *la tache* (the task), and to be paid by the day was a big step up.

But the family didn't *see* most of the money Garfield's father earned. Instead, they had credit at the plantation store for their basic living needs. And they also used tokens (the official plantation currency) to make small, every-day purchases. During harvesting time, when the sugarcane was cut and brought to the mill to extract the juice (by "grinding" it through a series of huge rollers), Garfield's father worked in the sugar house. He did 12-hour shifts every day for four months, noon to midnight. That allowed him to earn more

*Capt. Garfield Keller
and me at one of our
Creole dinners.*

money, and at the end of the grinding season, in January, he paid off any credit that had piled up over the course of the year. If there was some money left over, it was given to him in cash rather than tokens. This was the money Mr. Keller could "put away for a rainy day," said his son.

The plantation was almost completely self-sufficient, and the workers grew most of what they consumed in small garden plots near their houses. They kept chickens and ducks, and raised hogs which they butchered every winter to make cooking-lard and salt meat. They got sugar, cane syrup, and molasses from the sugarhouse. Plus, Garfield's father and his friends were good hunters and trappers, so as far as their food was concerned, they felt they wanted for nothing. "Well," Garfield said ruefully, "we really didn't know what was available in the outside world. The plantation was the whole universe as far as we were concerned."

*

Sicknesses were treated with local remedies, and there also were healers (*traiteurs*) who were reputed to be able to make maladies go away.

"If you needed a doctor, oh boy, that was a rough one," Garfield told me. "There was only one doctor for us in the whole area. He made his rounds weekly, and if you had illness in your family, you'd put a white flag on your gate. We didn't have cash to pay for doctors though, so most of the time we'd barter: give him something from the garden or pantry. Smoked sausages, wild game…"

At the time he was growing up (and until 1950), you couldn't phone a doctor either because there were no telephones. If you really needed to call someone "away," say in New Orleans (and of course that was only in dire emergencies), you would usually be calling Charity Hospital. "Seems like we had relatives or friends in there all the time," said Garfield. To make a call, you had to go to the Service Inn Café in Front Vacherie, which had the only telephone in town. (The café was near the railroad tracks so they were probably tapped into one of the telephone lines that paralleled the tracks.) "Of course, we couldn't go *into* the Service Inn to make our calls. When Black folks needed the phone, they had to stand by the side of the café near where the boss had his office, and he'd pass the phone to us through the window. Strange but true."

*

There was a small elementary school about a half-mile from the plantation, but it was for Whites only. Eventually the Parish authorities arranged for an elementary school for Blacks, but it was situated about a mile farther away than the

White school. That meant the walk to school for Blacks took about one hour each way. Garfield explains, "The White kids on the plantation had a bus which would take them back and forth. But we had to walk, and we walked almost twice as far as they rode."

Now, think about this: the kids on the plantation, Black and White, knew each other very well, played together all the time, hunted and fished together, and of course worked in the fields together, but when it came time for school, the White kids rode and the Black kids walked.

Everything at the Black school was hand-me-down: the blackboards, the desks, the school books. As new books were provided to the White kids, the used books were passed down to the Black children. "We knew whose old books we had received," said Garfield. "Sometimes we would even show our White friends on the plantation their names in the books we had been given."

*

There was a White man in the community, Garfield remembers, a Mr. Servais, who had a truck which he used to transport people to work in New Orleans, and when he could, he had his driver schedule his departure so that it would coincide with the Black kids' dismissal from school. That way, the kids could hop into the back of that truck and get a lift home.

"A minor thing for some perhaps," said Garfield, "but a huge help for us. Mr. Servais was very interested in giving us a break. So, as they say: 'There's a little good in the worst of us and there's a little bad in the best of us.' That's the deal with me. I see all of that. I don't see just one side of it. I see the whole thing. This man had his truck leave at a particular time so the driver could pick us up and bring us as far as his run. And that's how much less we had to walk."

Garfield sometimes actually waxes nostalgic for some of the better qualities of life during his youth on the plantation. "The strange thing is, we had no hard feelings toward our White counterparts. I guess we were accustomed to things as they were and just...just..." His voice trailed off for a moment, and then he added, "Those were the days, you know. Strange as it may seem now, we kids had a good relationship on the plantation with everyone. Every older person was called Mr. or Mrs., whether it was the Black children talking to White elders or the other way around." Remembering that show of respect for adults, a form of good manners that crossed race barriers when he was a child, seemed to please him.

*

There was a kind of social distancing required of Blacks in many places in those days, including grocery stores. Most grocery stores and bars were White-owned. Blacks could go into those stores, but not into the bar areas. Some had a little place in the back for Blacks only. Several stores had a counter on one end where people could order food and sundries, with the bar opposite. Blacks were only permitted to go up to the grocery counter to buy what they needed, and then they had to go back out to the street again. They were not allowed to turn around and look at the people inside, not permitted to address them or talk with them, even if they knew each other from outside. Even if they worked together every day, or played together on the plantation. Basically, in the White stores Blacks had to act as if they didn't know the Whites.

Some stores had a dance hall attached to the grocery and Blacks had to tread extra carefully when they went into those stores, especially on weekends when the white couples were there enjoying themselves. It was considered highly inappropriate to be observed by Blacks when doing something as intimate as dancing. "There was one grocery store that had a dance hall," Garfield remembers, "and one weekend, I went in there to get something. I had just forgotten what day it was. Saturday. Of course, I was ushered out right away."

*

Garfield's family attended the local Catholic church. The priest was Father Delnom, from France, a very sick man — what the modern world calls "abusive in the extreme."

"He was rough on everybody," Garfield says, "he obeyed the law, you know, the white/black thing — though I don't think he agreed with it. But, no, he didn't discriminate in his roughness — he gave equally harsh treatment to White and Black; he didn't discriminate in that area."

*

In the army, what was the most difficult thing for Garfield to accept when he was stationed at Fort Hood in Killeen, Texas, during segregation, was that sometimes there were visitors from the Soviet Union, or Soviet allies from Eastern Europe.

"They were our enemies and yet they had access to any-thing in Killeen: bars, restaurants and so on," he laments, "while we Blacks did not have that access! And we wore the uniform of our country! It was hard to accept that."

After three years in Germany, a place where no discrim-ination was practiced, Garfield came back to the U.S. The Deep South was a bit of a shock to him. Attitudes were changing for the better, some of the racism was disappearing, and the line between Blacks and Whites was not quite as pronounced, but it was still several years before the Civil Rights Acts would be passed. Our community in southern Louisiana was still strictly segregated. "Even so, I was happy to be home with my family," Garfield recalls.

One of Garfield's first jobs after he got out of the Army was at Oak Alley Plantation in Vacherie, a cattle ranch. He had worked there doing odd jobs before joining the service, and some months after he returned, the overseer, Paul Ory, con-tacted him and said he'd like to have Garfield back.

"He was a rough guy, a cowboy," Garfield said, "He was rough, period. But maybe I'm being too hard on him; he did have some good qualities. I learned lot from him, just working together..."

Of course, the overseer was a prejudiced man. But there were qualities in him that Garfield found outstanding. For instance, when he sent Garfield out to purchase things, he'd give him a blank check.

"Sometimes his wife or kids went along for the ride to New Orleans, but I was always in charge of looking after them, and in charge of the money. He trusted me. As a matter of fact, he was one of the few White people I knew who was able to make the fine distinction between segregation and business."

Apparently, the overseer trusted Garfield with his kids, too. Garfield would take them to the movies, for example, but of course they did not sit together because the theater was segregated. Garfield was upstairs on the balcony and they were downstairs. Still, the overseer's children were put in his care, and he felt honored by that. "My boss was not a man to trust people easily, you know, so I really appreciated that he trusted me so completely."

He also gave Garfield the job of chauffeuring Mrs. Andrew Stewart around — the plantation owner. Garfield became her personal driver. "Mrs. Stewart appreciated me a lot, and I appreciated her. We worked well together." I had the impression that, just as in the film, *Driving Miss Daisy*, Garfield became real friends with Gertrude Stewart. When influential White people like Mr. Ory and Mrs. Stewart expressed respect for Garfield, surely that helped him develop his self-esteem.

*

A few years later, Garfield was hired by the sheriff's department as a deputy sheriff. For that job, he had to share a police car with three other Black deputies, while the White deputies each had his own car. Fortunately, the department eventually changed to the point where each deputy was assigned his own area to patrol, and Garfield got his own cruiser.

"Life changes. Attitudes change," he says, "and at the end of my career, I was in charge of all the deputies — Black and White."

Reflecting on the journey from being born Black and poor on a sugar plantation during segregation, to the final accomplishment of his career — commanding all the deputies in the

Parish — he says, "I feel some measure of satisfaction. I have no remorse. I had no malice toward people, so that made it very easy for me, because I didn't go in with a chip on my shoulder. I heard a statement about being profiled — and it was a Black man who said this to me — he said, 'Well, aren't you...?' Meaning: aren't you profiling us Blacks? And I said, 'I'm an adult. A grownup. I have a job to do. I treat everyone equally.' That was my attitude," he went on, "I can't let all of the little things bother me. It wasn't difficult for me to defend or protect my enemies. I had no problem with that."

*

At one time, one of his bosses was Joe Nassar, who had been elected High Sheriff. They had a rough time starting off. Nassar needed to get Garfield's measure.

"But you know," Garfield says now, "Joe Nassar, even though we started rough, he's the one who promoted me to the highest rank — Chief Deputy. He made a statement before he died that that was the best move he ever made. I had the highest respect for him."

Largely, Garfield looks back on his life with gratitude: "I've been helped along the way. I've been helped tremendously by Blacks. But I've been helped tremendously by Whites as well. So, I look back now and that's the satisfaction I have, and why I have an attitude of malice toward none. I accepted that racism and segregation were the facts in those days, and I took it in stride. I have no regrets. None. No regrets at all. Thank God I was the victim not the perpetrator. You see, if there's anything bad to remember, it's on their conscience not mine."

*Sgt. Garfield at his Army base in Germany,
leaning against a ton-and-a-half truck, 1957.
He was in charge of the motor pool.*

Colored Girls Don't Have Wings

Imelda Oubre is the daughter of Miss Payne, the school principal and social activist and our neighbor from across the road. A few years ago, Imelda told me about the day the evils of segregation were brought home to her with an appalling event at church.

One Sunday morning when she was seven years old, her father took her to make her First Communion at morning Mass at St. Philip Catholic Church in Front Vacherie. Her family was living nearby in Wallace at the time, and that was their parish church. That same afternoon he took her back to church for *The Crowning of the Blessed Mother*.

The Black girls all wore flower wreaths on their heads for that celebration. But when Imelda walked up to the old, wooden gate in front of the church, she saw all the White girls at the front of the line wearing angel wings, covered in silver and gold glitter. Large wings, attached to the backs of their dresses.

Imelda looked up at her dad and asked, "Where are *my* wings?"

"Sweetie..." he answered with a sad look, "Colored girls don't have wings."

Then he squeezed her hand a little bit tighter and led her on into the church.

When she got home after the services, Imelda told her mother in a despondent voice about the second painful event of the day, "We had our pretty wreaths...but when we left church they took them from us."

That she had no angel wings that day may sound like a small thing to a grownup, but to a vulnerable little girl, "It was very hurting," she said. "I still think about it occasionally. But the Lord has blessed me so much that I don't feel any resentment toward people of another color now. I'm just thankful my children didn't have to go through those times."

Imelda Oubre Gros as a young lady.

IN THE PACIFIC

KAMIKAZE RAID

Uncle John Reulet lived in Baton Rouge, and in his retirement, he frequently made the one-hour trip to Vacherie to see family and friends. He'd often time his arrival at our house to be around the noon hour in case Mama had something good on the stove. John loved down-home Creole cooking. And when any of the Reulet brothers and sisters got together there was always stimulating conversation.

I remember one memorable day when the discussion got around to WWII. Three of his sisters were with us: Mama, Marjorie, and Janice. Aunt Janice said her husband's unit received a presidential citation for the Battle of the Bulge, and John told us his ship received two citations for heroic action.

John had served in the Navy in World War II as a gunner's mate on a ship in the South Pacific, where he was awarded a Purple Heart for injuries he sustained when a Japanese kamikaze plane crashed into his ship. His mate on the deck next to him, Seaman Tedesco, was killed in that action *(see adjoining picture)*. He said that he could still clearly picture the face of the Japanese pilot in the cockpit more than 70 years later.

During his time of service in the Pacific his naval task force made six amphibious landings, fighting to recapture a string of islands from the Japanese on "The Road to Tokyo."

John and Tedesco at the station on the ship.

I asked him for the name of his ship and then Googled it. On the official US Navy site, a picture came up of John with his mate, Seaman Tedesco. They were cradling two little dogs, Seven and Zero (after the ship LCI-G-70.) John said that he and several crew members had been washed ashore during a typhoon, and that's where they found the puppies. They brought them on board, but Seven fell overboard a few days later and eventually the commanding officer found out about Zero, and they had to bring it ashore.

Later on a Pacific island John ran into a high-school classmate, Marcel Graugnard, who was serving as an officer in the Navy. What would be the odds of two pals meeting accidently in the vast Pacific Ocean? And during a war?

Marcel told John that he'd like to get together later that day because as an officer he had access to "liquid refreshments." So, they met that evening in Marcel's quarters, and he broke out a bottle of Scotch, as promised, and they spent an unforgettable evening drinking highballs and reminiscing of home. John remembers that encounter fondly, if a bit hazy.

Pépère shouldering John's seabag the day he left for the Pacific theater. John doesn't look too happy. On the right, cousin Edwin Reulet who became an air ace in the Pacific war.

TWO BROTHERS

That day Uncle John came to lunch (see previous Kamikaze story), he told us of the time when he and his brother Woodrow, who was a few years older, met in the Pacific theatre during WWII.

Wood was in the Army Air Forces, and hop-scotched around the battle zones ferrying supplies to US troops. At a stop on Moratai Island, he spotted a ship anchored in the distance which had the number 70 on it, and that was exciting, because he knew from his correspondence with his brother John that 70 was the number of his ship.

Fortunately, Wood then met a sailor who was manning a signaling post sending messages from the shore to the ship via Morse Code, using flashing light signals, and he asked him to inquire if John Reulet was onboard. The response: Affirmative. He then asked if John could meet him on shore. The response: Negative.

Tec. Sgt Wood Reulet ready for a short ride to the Vacherie train station, shipping out to the Pacific.

At that point, Wood took it upon himself to go out to the ship. He commandeered a native outrigger canoe in which he was paddled to the vessel, then was hoisted on board. He was only allowed to visit with John for 15 minutes before being sent back to shore, but it was a memorable moment for the two bothers. (Later in the war, they managed to meet up again on a different Pacific island, where they had a proper reunion.)

Last surviving Reulet family members at John's 90th birthday party, 2014. Aunt Janice, Uncle Wood, Uncle John, Aunt Marjorie

PEOPLE OF COLOR

COLORED FOLKS

The first "colored" person I ever knew was Boy Isom, who lived across the road from us. His given name was Elie, and it's not difficult to imagine how he acquired that nickname. But everyone, his children — even his wife — called him "Boy." (He called her, "Madame Boy.")

Boy was Pépère Victor's faithful handyman and friend, always available when my grandfather needed help to do some chore in the yard or work with the cattle, digging post holes, repairing the fences, and so on. I don't remember the first time I met him; as far as I was concerned, Boy had always been with us. As natural a part of our landscape as anyone.

He lived across the road in Uncle Jean Reulet's house. Jean had passed away back in the late 1920s, and his five unmarried daughters had moved to New Orleans to work with the Archdiocese, mainly serving priests as cleaning ladies and cooks. When the youngest sister made her move to the city, the five siblings decided to let Boy use the house and property until they returned to Vacherie in retirement. (He had been *their* handyman, too.)

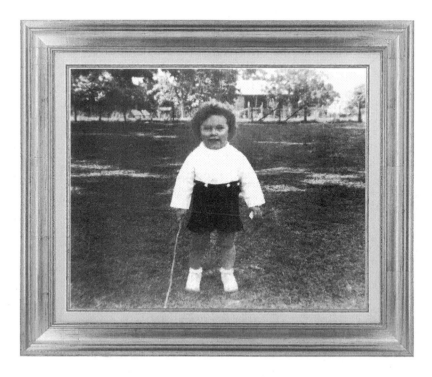

Aside from showing 3-year-old bushy-haired me here, this is the only photo we have of Boy's house and his large yard, in the background, which was situated directly across the road from us.

After living all his life in plantation shacks, scratching out a meager living for his family behind a mule-drawn plow, Boy suddenly found himself master of a substantial plot of land with a large house, barns and outbuildings, pastures, and space for a large vegetable garden. His front yard had a huge Magnolia tree in it, which is still standing today. It was as if Boy had managed — magically — to beat the system!

Boy was a strapping man of about 6' 2", and he had an older brother who was even bigger and taller than him. People called his brother Man. Boy and Man. Man and Boy. A wonderful tandem.

Man worked a few miles away on Armant Plantation. There was a popular story that circulated featuring Man and Mr. Tucker, his boss. I heard it many times, and sometimes I'd ask Boy to retell it, because hearing the story in Creole added an even more colorful dimension to it.

Mister Tucker (as everyone referred to him, even when speaking French) was from Arkansas (Argenta, I believe), and had come to Vacherie to manage the plantation and the sugar house. As the story goes, one Sunday afternoon, Man took a horse-drawn buggy belonging to Tucker and treated himself to a leisurely ride through the fields behind the sugar house. The boss was away in New Orleans on business so apparently Man felt he could get away with this little self-indulgence. The buggy was new and intended for use only to ferry the family to church or to take the ladies out on evening rides.

Man was feeling good. He had a flask of Muscatel with him, and was gaily swigging it down when surprise — *Wa be da Boom!* — he ran into Mr. Tucker at a crossroad in the field! Tucker had come home early and was riding around in his truck, checking on the sugar cane.

Tucker braked hard ("Li a brake sec!" as Boy said in Creole) and furiously motioned for Man to get off the buggy. Then he started yelling, grabbed Man's horse whip, and attempted to beat him with it. Well, Man was a big fellow, as I mentioned; he towered over his boss and easily wrapped his enormous arms around Tucker to immobilize him. Of course, he knew if he actually struck Tucker — a White man and his boss, a double whammy — that there could be very serious consequences.

So, he just tried to restrain Tucker until his anger ebbed and he could come to his senses.

Unfortunately, however, Tucker had a small dog in the truck which jumped out and started barking at Man and nipping at his ankles. A few people who witnessed the fracas from afar said that Man would let go of Tucker for a second to shoo the dog, then grab Tucker again, then shoo the dog again, then grab Tucker again...and that ballet lasted for several minutes, until Tucker ended it by saying, "Well, all right, Man. All right. But just don't do it again. Okay?"

Tucker surely knew that in terms of sheer physical strength, he had been beaten. But he let Man save face, too, without dolling out serious reproach or punishment for taking the buggy without permission. From that moment on, Tucker and Man became the best of friends, and Man could get pretty much anything he wanted out of Tucker.

Not surprisingly, Boy loved to tell this story, about how his big brother had given "Meester" Tucker his well-deserved comeuppance.

Now, as I was saying, Boy lived with his large family rent-free on the homestead of Uncle Jean Reulet. He must have been the envy of his peers. Surely for the first time in his life he felt he was somebody. But at the time he couldn't know when the Reulet sisters would return, there was always the specter hanging over him that he could lose his home, and then where would he go?

Well, I found the answer to that conundrum a few years ago when I went to the courthouse to look up some documents for this book. While roaming the stacks in the archives, I spied a property transfer dossier in the name of Elie Isom, Boy's name. I was curious, so I paid the requisite dollar-per-page for a copy of the file.

I read it carefully when I got home, and it was apparent that Boy had been painfully aware of his uncertain situation, and deeply concerned that he could find himself on the street should the owners of the house return, and I was amazed, given his situation in life, that he had had the wherewithal to do something about it.

With money he had scrimped and saved throughout his life doing odd jobs and selling eggs, chickens, and produce, Boy bought a large old house a few miles away, for the then-hefty sum of $900. Owning that house gave him peace of mind. It was his insurance that, should that fateful day arrive when the Reulet sisters returned, he was protected. Fortunately, they remained in New Orleans, and we continued to enjoy Boy's company and friendship until the day he died — in the house on the Reulet property where he lived for over 30 years.

*

There is one African American I do recall meeting for the first time — a wonderful man called Lloyd Jessie. Lloyd had a big family and rented a house from Aunt Marie Reulet at the end of her pasture. It was only a cabin really, and not in the best state of repair. Then again, the rent was negligible.

Before he started paying rent there, Lloyd enjoyed the use of the cabin as part of his remuneration when he worked for Aunt Marie's uncles Tétin and Jean. When her uncles died, the land was rented out to the Kliebert brothers of Molaison. Lloyd continued working there, but for new bosses. During that time, Aunt Marie let him stay put in the cabin for the nominal sum of five dollars per month.

One summer afternoon, when I was about five, we were sitting on Aunt Marie's back steps, having just come from picking tomatoes, when I saw a man in the distance leaving the cabin and walking in our direction. But instead of coming to the side entrance, which was the most direct route, he took the roundabout way through the pasture, ending up at Aunt Marie's back gate. I didn't realize it at the time, but Lloyd was well versed in Black/White protocol: the back door was the shortest distance to a White person's heart.

We went to meet him at the gate, and I particularly remember him addressing my aunt as "Mamzelle Marie," a new word for me. He was being polite, even deferential. "Mamzelle" is Creole for *Mademoiselle*, and since Aunt Marie had never married, she was rightly addressed as "Mamzelle."

The reason Lloyd came over was to ask Marie if he could defer paying rent for that month until work picked up. He said it was hard to make ends meet during the slow summer season, but the sugarcane harvest would soon be coming, and he promised he would give her the money in arrears. Aunt Marie listened with an understanding demeanor. Then she reached out and took his hand from across the fence and squeezed it hard, saying, "Lloyd, you gave faithful service to my uncles. Don't worry about the rent for the next few months. Let us just forget about it."

I thought she was the most generous person in the world, letting go of that money just like that. And Lloyd's gratitude to her overflowed in his eyes and smile.

No doubt about it, Lloyd was an exceptionally warm person. A sincerely caring person. He spoke with such interest in the little boy that I was. I have never forgotten him. It wasn't all that common to have grown-ups ask me questions and then really listen to my responses. But he did. He convinced me that what I thought and felt was of real interest to him. Lloyd was that kind of person.

Some years later, he moved to Jessietown, where he built a small house — a home of his own. When I was a young teenager, I used to ride my bike around that area, and every time I'd see him, he'd call, "*Hey there, Colin.*" Usually, he spotted me from his front porch, where he spent summer afternoons during the months when field work stopped around 10 a.m. because the heat was too intense. Often, I'd stop at his gate to chat for a few minutes. I sensed a special bond between us, because he'd been so kind to me when I was very young, and like all human beings, whatever happens when we're very young leaves a mark on us — for good or ill — in this case for good, of course. Lloyd Jessie marked me with his kindness. His humanity. And I'm grateful for that mark to this day.

BLACK VISITORS
AUGUST, 1949

For many of us who grew up under segregation, it's difficult to remember when we first became aware of the system that mandated separation of the races. I probably noticed its sometimes-subtle rules at church, because the "colored people" were relegated to a "Reserved" section in the back. In addition, they had to wait until every White person had been served before they could go to the front of the church to receive Communion. Even a child would not have missed the signal there!

Of course, just listening to adults talk at a time when most held negative views of African Americans, and were not shy in letting other people know it, was one of the most important ways the message, *"Blacks are inferior,"* was passed on. By the age of three or four, the "rightness" of segregation was imprinted on young people's minds — and that was that. No one I knew ever questioned the beliefs and behaviors we were conditioned to assume about race. We just accepted segregation as an inviolable fact of life.

However, when I was seven, I witnessed an incident that changed me and informed my feelings and relationships with African Americans for the rest of my life. By way of introduction to the story, you need to know that my father had recently been appointed to the School Board.

The event took place on a stifling summer evening in late August, a few days before the beginning of the schoolyear. Daddy and I were working on an extension of the house, to accommodate the children in our growing family. Mary had been born a few months before, and Margaret and Jude would be arriving in the next few years.

We were at work on the new back bedroom, with the help of Lloyd Clement. Lloyd had been a POW in Germany and had taken up the carpentry trade on the G.I. Bill after his return. He'd already put up the frame and roof, and we were now closing in the rooms and installing the floor before the cold weather arrived.

The outer wall on the east side was not yet closed in, only the upright 2 x 4's were in place, and the "floor" consisted of parallel joists, 18 inches apart and two feet off the ground. (Houses in Vacherie were raised then.) We were standing on bare ground to nail in the floorboards, cutting each board with a hand saw as we went along, and it was slow going. Daddy did most of the sawing, using the floor joists as saw-horses. He had me hold the end that was to be discarded, and now and then he'd also let me drive in a few easy nails.

At one point, while Daddy was occupied sawing a board, I looked through the uprights of the open wall and saw five "colored people" coming toward us — three women and two men — all neatly dressed, the men in coat and tie. They had arrived from the side road that is Pine Street today, then an unpaved lane. It was unusual for us to have visitors at that time of day, and more unusual to have Black visitors.

When they got to us, the apparent leader said, "Good evening, Mr. Paul," in a friendly but firm voice. I recognized her as our neighbor from across the road, a woman we knew as Madame Wilbotte, whose professional name as a school principal was Miss Payne.

Daddy was startled. He looked at the group briefly, then went back to his sawing, taking his good old time. After a while, he glanced up again and greeted them in an unusually offhanded way for him — just a brief, "Hallo," followed by mumbling that we were hurrying to finish the floor and walls. The truth is, he didn't look too pleased to have these visitors. He grabbed another board, measured it, motioned me to hold the end steady as usual, and started sawing.

I was puzzled. *What do these people want? And why is Daddy not being his usual friendly self?* My father normally had a friendly and easygoing manner with Blacks. But not today. My eyes darted from them, to him, and back again. I just couldn't figure out why they were there or why Daddy wasn't more forthcoming.

The visitors waited to let Daddy finish nailing the second board in place, and then Miss Payne spoke: "Mr. Paul, we've come to talk to you about Shell Mound School."

"Yeah?" my father said, looking up from his work. "What is it exactly?"

Things were starting to become clearer for me; Daddy was being shoehorned into an uncomfortable position.

"We came to see you as our new School Board member. There are some things we would appreciate you looking into for us."

I noticed how non-demanding she sounded when she listed her grievances, how non-threatening she was in spite of the gravity in her voice, and how the other visitors were looking on in a similar, friendly manner. By that time, of course, experience had taught Blacks how to *play* Whites, according to the demands of various situations. Three hundred and fifty years of slavery and Jim Crow had taught them how to work it when they were obliged to approach White people *hat in hand*. They knew to use the back door, to be friendly and polite, to dress well, to remain calm, to smile.

SCHOOL DAYS 1953-'54
Shell Mound Elem.

Miss Payne, school principal.

It's amazing what a seven-year-old can understand; even before Miss Payne listed all the things they wanted fixed, I knew what this was about. During the past school year, I'd seen the Black children walking to school while the White kids rode the bus. I'd also seen something else even more disturbing: some older boys on our bus threw rocks at the "colored" children when we passed them walking home after school. I remembered how that disturbed me, how it churned my stomach and hurt my heart. And I remembered how Mama reacted when I told her about it, "We can't do anything about that," she said sadly, "if we complain, the White people will start throwing rocks at *us*. We just have to hope for the best."

I had the impression, seeing the quandary Daddy was getting into, that if by the wave of a magic wand he could have been physically transported away from this situation, he would have been a happy man. But he couldn't wish the situation away. He was on the School Board. He had responsibilities. He had to deal with it in the here and now.

At this point in his life, I don't believe he was any more enlightened on the subject of race than his peers in the community. My father was a product of his times, and even if he had been open to providing Blacks more help than was deemed necessary by his fellow Board members, he would probably not have succeeded. In those local governing bodies, you had to *Go along to get along*. The Board had its policies on the subject of race, and my father adhered to them. Now, was he comfortable with that deep down? Impossible to say because we never talked about it. And that, too – *not* talking about troubling things — was typical for those times.

Miss Payne, as principal of Shell Mound School, was jeopardizing her teaching career by asking for changes. She could have been demoted to simple teacher at the Board's whim, with a corresponding drop in salary, had this confrontation turned ugly. She knew very well that this "friendly" meeting could have had negative consequences for her, but she was courageous enough to try to do something for her people.

She opened her argument by saying that they were not asking to overturn a situation that was codified by law and custom. In that approach, she was following *the rules of engagement* to the letter; presenting a non-threatening, non-demanding demeanor was Rule No. 1. Miss Payne was expert at that role. She insisted that they only wanted a few *adjustments* — "to help the children."

The school plant, if it could be called that in its dilapidated condition, was being moved from mid-Back Vacherie (present day Palm Street) to a site near Golden Star Plantation, about a mile to the east, which would result in double the walking distance for those children who lived on Coteau Plantation, or elsewhere in West Vacherie. Miss Payne asked if they could possibly have some bus transportation, and even added that they weren't asking for a *new* bus — a secondhand bus would do just fine.

Daddy professed to be unaware of any new busses for the parish, and was noncommittal.

"Well, yeah, if we can do that, we'll try." Not the answer Miss Payne and her colleagues were waiting to hear. But when she asked if some minor improvements could be made in the new school, such as putting up a wall to separate two classrooms, and installing better lavatory facilities, he gave her a firm, "Yes." Truth is, a crew was already at work on the school, and the improvements she requested could be accomplished rapidly and at no extra cost.

Then there was the question of school lunches. In the academic year just past, school lunches were free, thanks to Governor Earl Long, who had made good on one of his campaign promises.

"That would be a good thing to do," Daddy said about the lunchroom, "but with the new school being readied, I don't know if the budget will stretch that far..."

Of course, Black people were used to hearing talk of "budgetary restraints," and from the look on her face, I understood Miss Payne didn't believe her lunchroom would be a reality any time soon.

Next, she brought up the subject of books and desks, which were, "...in a deplorable condition, and in some cases non-existent." She pointed out that you can't expect children to learn if they have to share a book with three or four other kids.

Daddy made a few noises about remedying that situation, but was noncommittal again.

I'm pretty sure he was thinking, *What did I get myself into by joining the Board?*

Although that impromptu meeting did not last more than 15 minutes, sometime during the school year, the Blacks received our old school bus — the pre-war one with lateral seats. And the following summer, I went with Daddy to the school to inspect the new lunchroom facilities being built. Not exactly a 3-star restaurant, but a definite improvement on the old Palm Street facility.

It was evident from their body language that Miss Payne and the other visitors were not enthusiastic about the results of the meeting. But they seemed to take pains not to let their true feelings show — not too much, anyway — just enough to get the message across without seeming to be ungrateful. There would be other meetings in the future, and they needed to keep the lines of communication open.

Miss Payne had one last thing to say, and she stated it with a flourish: "Mr. Paul, this man next to me was recently honorably discharged from the United States Army. He served his country for ten years, and he saw action in Normandy. Don't you think his children deserve better than what they're getting?"

Well, that knocked the wind out of everybody.

Miss Payne threw her head back, as if the closing statement she had just given (which was well prepared and flawlessly delivered) had conveyed the exact effect she was looking for. All eyes were directed to the ex-soldier, then to Daddy for his answer. "I believe you're right," is all he could say. There was no other appropriate response. Then they shook hands all around, and shook mine, too, and headed back from whence they'd come.

Miss Payne at 90.

CREOLE SUMMIT

"Vacherie resident hosts monthly Creole get-together"

By Pam Folse, *The News-Examiner-Enterprise,*

JANUARY 2015

From left: John Gros, Elray Oubre, August Baptiste,
Colin Gravois, Garfield Keller, Lawrence Keller.

All of the identified Creole speakers in Vacherie are invited to share a meal and conversation at the home of Colin Gravois. This month's "summit" was attended by Elray Oubre, August Baptiste, Garfield Keller, Lawrence Keller, and John Gros.

At the monthly gathering, the men speak only Creole. The youngest in attendance was in his mid-50s and the senior member was in his 80s.

Gravois, who maintains dual residency in Vacherie and Paris, said the group is doing what it can to preserve their local heritage.

The group meets when he is in Vacherie, and they began meeting a few years ago when Baptiste and Lawrence Keller made repairs to his house. Others were invited over the years.

Gravois, along with Creole speakers Morrison Narcisse and Horace Domino, travelled to New Roads in 2012 and met with a Creole group there. They so enjoyed the hospitality shown to them that they invited the group to come to Vacherie.

The New Roads group accepted the invitation and came by bus to Lake Des Allemands where they were treated to a traditional Vacherie meal. The two groups enjoyed speaking Creole together, and the Vacherie folks were entertained by the New Roads group, whose members sang spirituals in Creole.

At this month's summit, the men told stories, shared experiences and were very grateful to have the opportunity to spend time with one another. They also enjoyed the delicious meal of seafood gumbo, salad and apple pie which Gravois prepared for them. The group is open to other members and the only rule is that participants must talk Creole when they can.

Gravois speaks several dialects of Creole: Vacherie Creole, Creole spoken in the St. Martinville and Breaux Bridge area, as well as the version used in the New Roads. According to him, "Any Creole is better than no Creole at all."

Creole Summit lunch, 2016. From left: Capt. Keller, Lawrence Keller, John Gros, Elray Oubre, and August Baptiste.

ARMY DAYS

October 1966, Germany

It's October 10, 1966, a bright sunny day. I'm on a train heading north from Frankfurt to a town called *Moenchengladbach* — as best as I can make out from the name on my ticket; German writing is hard to decipher.

I am the only U.S. Army person in that railcar and I'm in uniform, right in the middle of a group of Germans, and I'm wondering how they feel about me, an American soldier whose Army defeated them just 20 years ago. I'm sure most of them lost loved ones in that conflict. *What are they thinking?*

And what scenery. The tracks run along the Rhine River, hugging the right bank going downstream to Rotterdam in the Netherlands (if I remember my high school geography). The day is glorious. Clear skies, sun shining brightly,

Freshly minted Army Private, Fort Polk, Louisiana, March 1966.

medieval castles perched on high here and there on each side of the river, vineyards rising steeply up the banks, workers busy picking grapes. The river traffic is mostly barges pushed by tugs, like on our Mississippi back home, and now and then a sightseeing boat glides by. A wonderful introduction to Germany. I'm feeling good. If this is a dream, don't wake me up.

Let us back up a little here. After basic training at Fort Polk, Louisiana, and advanced training at Fort Benjamin Harrison near Indianapolis, we shipped out to Germany from McGuire AFB in New Jersey. We spent one overnight in Frankfurt on arrival, and then we were sent out to our final postings. The Transit Office at the Frankfurt train station put a ticket in my hand and said I would be going north to Moenchengladbach. At that point of the trip, with little sleep for the past several days, Moenchengladbach or the moon meant the same to me.

Back to the train, I engage a few people in conversation, and I am happy to see that they are friendly, and that some speak English so I can communicate easily. What I really want to know is when I will be disembarking. They said, "We have a long way to go, just relax."

By late afternoon, a gentleman seated next to me, with whom I earlier had an interesting chat about Germany, indicated that the next stop would be mine. I thanked him and readied my things for arrival, having been told by the Transit Office that someone from my unit would be waiting for me at the station, and not to worry: The Army takes care of its own.

Well, after some time searching the station in and out, I could find no one who looked anything like US Army personnel. It was getting late, and I was hungry, so I decided to have something to eat at the station restaurant and took a table from where I could survey the arrivals area in case someone showed up for me. I had a satisfying meal of scrambled eggs with ham and potato salad, a glass of beer (not chilled), and ice cream. Then I waited some more.

Just as I had decided to take a hotel room for the night, I saw some soldiers arriving in the station. They were not American looking, but I walked up to them anyway to ask if they knew of any US base in the area. They said they were British, and, yes, there was an American unit on their base. They had just come to bring a buddy to the station and were going right back and would take me with them, so we threw my baggage in the back of the Land Rover and hopped in for the ride to base.

The Brits were nice kids and had great-looking uniforms. Thick deep-green sweaters with leather shoulder and elbow patches, camo pants tucked into laced-up boots, airborne style, and black berets, even a scarf rakishly tied around their necks. That sure looked great compared to my rumpled dress greens after a week on the road, with that same shirt and tie from stateside.

I was all questions: where were we going, what kind of unit was it, what was the base like, that kind of thing. They said they didn't know much about the Americans, only that it was a very small unit and they would drop me off shortly; the ride only took about 20 minutes. They also informed me that we were situated on the British army HQ in Germany (official designation: British Army of the Rhine, or BAOR), which also served as a NATO base, with personnel from the UK, Belgium, the Netherlands, Germany, Canada, and a small US contingent. Sounded like it was going to be an exciting time in the old town already.

Leaving boot camp June 1966.

The more they told me, the "curious-er" and "curious-er" the situation was getting to be. I remember having the fleeting thoughts that just a short time before in the US, contemplating what a long troopship passage out of Oakland to Southeast Asia would be like, and, of course, what awaited me in Vietnam, and here I was less than 10 days later riding in a British army Land Rover in the dark of night with two Brit soldiers whom I had just met, to my new posting in northern Germany. Wrap your minds around that, if you please! Life, as the saying goes, is stranger than fiction.

At one point it looked like we were going through a modern-looking town when they informed me we were already on base. I had not noticed any guard posts or gates, but they told me it was an "open" base: People could come and go as they pleased, even German civilians, even Russian spies if there were any in the area.

A few moments later we pulled into the parking area of C Company where the Americans were situated. The Brits helped me carry my stuff into the barracks; they wanted to be sure that I would be taken care of for the night. On entering the building, we were confronted with a long corridor, doors on each side, all shut tight, with no names or indications of any sort. We studied the situation for a few seconds and decided to knock around randomly to see if we could find someone. At about the middle of the hallway, loud party noises were coming through a door on the left, so I knocked.

Inside, there was a group of about a dozen GIs having a ball. A poker game was in full swing in one corner, while other soldiers were cutting up around the room, drinking beer, laughing and kidding around. Of course, they stopped dead in their tracks when I opened the door, but when they realized after a few awkward moments that I was just a newcomer to the unit and not an inspector or such, they greeted me profusely and carried on as before.

I thanked the Brits for their help, wished them the best, then settled down with the American boys for a few beers. They answered some of my questions, and after a while issued me a bed.

I settled down for the night, reflecting on what a wild ride it had been since I left my base in the US. It was a long way from Back Vacherie, and I was going to have a full night's sleep for the first time in over a week.

*

I spent my first day at the office getting acquainted with the guys and some of the officers, learning the office setup and working conditions, where to get a sandwich, and other basics. I was assigned a desk, a typewriter, and a place to hang my hat; in the army, hats always had to be removed indoors.

Our hours were 8:15 to 5:15, and on my first day, after work, I decided to take a roundabout route back to the barracks. At lunch when I'd gone out with the boys for a sandwich at a British club near the office, I'd been surprised to see a number and variety of stores in a small shopping area close to HQ — some German-run, some Brit. I wanted to explore the place, so I told the guys I'd see them back in the barracks in about an hour.

After browsing a while, I arrived at a building called Cambridge House, which was the library and education center for the base. It was humming with activity as classes were in session. I saw a small poster advertising German lessons, and when I inquired at the reception desk, a woman told me that a class of beginners' German was starting in an hour. I signed up.

Me and my new Mercedes-Benz.

When I went back out into the hallway, I bumped into a professor named Sheila, from Northern Ireland, who was en route to her class: university-level History. We got to talking and I expressed interest in her subject. As she was currently teaching the American Revolution, she asked if I wanted to sit in on the class.

I found a place in the back of the room, and was soon enjoying a lecture on a subject I was at least as well, if not better, versed in than the teacher. She told the story of one of "the British heroes" of the Revolution — and you just can't make this up — her "hero" was Benedict Arnold!

When she asked the students for questions and no one came forward, I raised my hand. She said, "Oh, yes, we have a visitor today, Mr...Oh dear...Sorry! I didn't get your name." I filled her in. "Yes. Private Gravois from the American Army, of course. And what is your question?"

"Well," I said, "it's not a question. It's a statement of fact: General Arnold may be a hero to you British, but for us he was a traitor — and would have been shot if George Washington had gotten his hands on him."

Twenty pairs of eyes turned to look at me.

The teacher seemed a bit flummoxed, "Well, yes...Of course," she said, gracefully trying to build a bridge across the Atlantic, "There are often two sides to a story...and this is one of those occasions."

*

After challenging Sheila's view of a bonified British hero, I went to my German class. The teacher was a major in the German army on base — a nice guy and great teacher. German is not an easy language to learn, and his brief introduction on the different declensions of German verbs was complex enough to make me want to run. But I stayed the course.

After my German class, I arrived back at the barracks well past 9 p.m. — too late for supper. The guys were worried about me — thought I'd gotten lost and couldn't find my way back.

One guy with his own car had even gone out searching for me. But I reassured them I'd only been looking around the area, trying to get my bearings.

They were surprised to learn about Cambridge House, the library, and the free university-level classes, and I doubt if any one of them ever set foot in that place, even after I told them about it enthusiastically. It seemed to me that they simply had no interest in improving themselves; they were not curious. In fact, during their time in Germany, they rarely ventured beyond the base to see the surrounding area.

Some evenings, before I acquired a car, I would jump on the double-decker bus to town. The bus mainly served the German civilian workers on the base, of which there were hundreds: cleaning crews, grounds-keepers, the people who worked in British administrative units, and so on. Every day, *putzfraus*

(*putz*: cleaning / *fraus*: women) came by to clean the barracks and lavatories. (The British Army kindly relieved us of those classic GI chores.)

I went into town mainly to buy newspapers and magazines. The news vendor kept all back issues of the *New York Herald Tribune* and *The New York Times* for me. Then I'd treat myself to dinner at the train station or a nearby restaurant — nothing expensive, but good, solid fare. Usually, I got back to the barracks around 10:30 p.m. where I'd find the guys in the common room after their dinner in one of the British clubs. They'd be drinking beer and playing poker or dice, and sometimes I'd join in.

Once my Top-Secret clearance arrived, I was given a full briefing on our mission: In the event of an invasion of West Germany we were to deliver nuclear-tipped field artillery onto Russian tanks coming from East Germany. Remember: This was the height of the Cold War, and the Brits and Americans were there to protect West Germany from invasion from the Soviet bloc. The threat was very real, and *readiness* was the watchword throughout US forces in Germany.

Besides being the colonel's executive assistant, taking dictation and typing, my job also called for a variety of other "skills": welcoming visitors; placing and answering telephone calls; acting as the colonel's messenger. For example, he sent me to his house to pick up his service revolver on the day he left for training in Heidelberg. Another time he asked me to take 200 German marks to his wife for a shopping trip to Dusseldorf that she would be taking with other officers' wives. When I could have been shipped off to the jungles of Southeast Asia, I considered myself fortunate to be in such a comfortable post in Germany instead.

At one point, I took training in crypto operation (codes transmissions) — just in case one of the crypto men ever went missing for some reason; I could then fill in.

It interested me enormously to learn how secret messages were sent and received. We had a crypto room that was secured with double steel doors and a combination lock. Already our offices were located in a highly secure wing of the building, but we still couldn't take a chance on a break in. Those of you who are familiar with code breaking operations at

Bletchley Park in WWII will remember that the Enigma code machine used by the Germans was based on a system of rotors, four to six, with each rotor having all 26 letters of the alphabet and the digits 0 to 9 on it. Our machines were built on the same principle.

We received messages around the clock, some "in the clear" (not coded) and others coded. We also received one message daily with "the key" to use just for that day. The key enabled our machines to decode random blocks of letters. The constant flow of messages disguised any sudden spike in the number of real messages coming in — a spike which could tip off the enemy that things were heating up and could increase the chance of them reacting aggressively. Some messages were operational — meaning, we had to act on them. But we were always looking out for the really big message: "Lock and Load" which would indicate that we had to direct our subunits to arm the missiles and go into war mode immediately.

Fortunately, the "Lock and Load" message never arrived.

Our guys on the missile sites spread around northern Germany had to be in position to fire our missiles within an hour, and that degree of readiness was accomplished by monthly technical proficiency inspections. We had two sub-HQs which had final operational control of our firing units, but it was our responsibility to keep the whole theater of operations prepared for any eventuality. This was serious business, and everyone understood what was at stake.

As serious as the atmosphere was, however, once my duties were clearly defined everything went smoothly, and I relaxed into "cruise control." The colonel was a taskmaster but a fair one; it was a pleasure working with him. And the guys were fun to work with, too. We had a great team going.

*

On payday, in February, 1967, James Darden, our mail clerk, put his car, a 1959 Mercedes-Benz up for sale. He would be rotating back to the US in a few weeks and was in a hurry to get rid of it. There was an undetermined mechanical problem, and he didn't get any ready takers, so for $150, I decided to go for it. I had cash in hand and made him an offer he couldn't refuse — since no one else wanted to touch that car. I reasoned that if it turned out there was a major mechanical problem, I'd only be losing a negligible amount.

For repairs, Darden suggested I try Fritz, a junkyard mechanic in Wickrath, the next town over. He was already familiar with the car, so that night after work a friend towed me to his place. Fritz was our guys' first choice in repairs. They told me he not only gave good service but was inexpensive, too. Well, he did give good service — and cheap. For 600 Deutsche Marks (about $150) Fritz had me on the road within days. Now I was in for a total of $300, but that was nothing considering I drove that Benz for eight years, and it only needed a few repairs during that entire time. In fact, it turned out to be the best deal I ever made on an automobile. It took me all over Europe and the UK several times, and finally died a peaceful death in Paris, in 1975.

*

I have to admit, Army life was splendid for me personally. I have only wonderful memories of those 18 months in Germany and around Europe. It wasn't exactly a paid vacation, we did have to work, of course, but we had a lot of privileges. We were on our own from 5:15 in the afternoon until 8:15 the next morning, and that's a lot of free time. Plus, there were no inspections, no KP, no guard duty, no passes required to go off the base at night, and even better: we had weekends off except for a couple of times a year when we went on maneuvers.

Most of the officers were West Pointers and likeable guys. I worked closely with a captain who was a "good ole boy" from Yazoo City, Mississippi; he reminded me of home and we got on well. We were all on friendly terms, regardless of our backgrounds or rank, officers and enlisted men alike.

*

Since we were not more than 15 US personnel in the barracks and were stationed on a British base, we had no US Army mess hall, so we took our meals in teashops or British clubs or off base on the German economy. To compensate for the lack of eating facilities the Army gave us a *per diem* which amounted to around $300 a month (more than $2,000 in today's dollars), paid in cash on payday. One could eat three meals a day for much less than that, and that extra cash came in handy for other things, like buying a car and visits around Europe.

Most of us left the barracks in the morning without breakfast. But we knew that around 9 o'clock the NAAFI wagon (food cart) would pass through the halls and we could get hot drinks, pastries, and German *brotchen* (little breads). NAAFI (Navy Army Air Force Institute) is the British organization that supports service members and their families — the equivalent to our USO. And deep in the bowels of HQ building there was also a German café *snell imbiss* — fast food, German style. Plus, the NAAFI snack wagon passed again in the mid-afternoon, loaded with tea and cakes. So, all in all, no one went hungry.

When I was on a mission in the building, I would sometimes make a detour to the German café for a drink and to read the British papers. Other times, I would pass by the French liaison office to visit the two French guys, Jean-Bernard Vargues and Pierre Montet, who worked with their colonel there, or go see some Belgian friends in another part of the building, to speak some French, Belgian-style.

There were tight controls for everyone entering the HQ building, and then there was a second security point before one could access the restricted US Army area, where we handled Top Secret materials. Naturally, we got to know well the German and British soldiers manning that interior checkpoint. One of them was a German sergeant named Hans Jacobi, who was studying at night at a local university preparing for his transition to civilian life the following year. He wanted to finish the master's degree he'd put on hold when he joined the *Bundeswehr*, the German military.

One day Jacobi told me that the next week his class would be having a round-table discussion on post-WWII international politics, specifically German rearmament. Would I like to attend and speak to the class? I told him I would, and the following week I found myself in front of 15 of his fellow students, all serious, mature gentlemen (no women) in their late twenties and early thirties.

My impression is that most Germans then, and even today, were more pacifist than militarist, given how their country was destroyed in the War. They had grown up in its ruins and were acutely aware that the Marshall Plan and the CARE packages sent by the U.S. had helped them get back on their feet. Thankful for that, they harbored no ill feeling toward Americans that I could tell. I was warmly received and we had a fruitful 90-minute Q & A session.

A bit nervous at first about what they would throw at me, it took me a few minutes to get settled, but from that point on I held my own well.

The first question was: "Isn't the U.S. involved in Vietnam just to help the economy at home?"

For a moment, I was stumped for an answer, then it came to me that the post-war economy in the U.S. rode one of the greatest economic booms in the country's history — and we were at peace. That answer more than satisfied them, and from then on, the give-and-take was very friendly.

I stayed after class to have a chat with the teacher, a German woman in her 50s. Friendly, with a sharp mind. Her English was impeccable, so much so that when she pulled out a book by someone she described as one of her favorite writers, I saw it was by the American, James Thurber, *My Life and Hard Times* — one of my all-time favorites, too.

It may not sound like much to share love for a particular book with a German, but during the War, a lot of people on the Allied side believed Germans were nothing but a pack of evil monsters, responsible for millions of human beings being tortured, starved, and gassed. Yet, only 20 years later, here we were — a few individuals of good will — forging toward some kind of humanity with each other. Former enemies, finding common ground.

HERE AND THERE

VICTOR DOES HIS BIT

In 1948, newly-elected Governor Earl Long of Louisiana made a major push to register African Americans on the voting rolls. That was 17 years prior to the 1965 Voting Rights Act. My grandfather, Victor Reulet, in his position as assistant registrar of voters, was in the middle of it all. That was a part-time job (as was typical in those days for registrars) performed out of the St James Parish courthouse.

An admirer of the 45th governor of the state, Victor took at heart Long's admonition to the registrars of Louisiana to "abolish voting roadblocks," and did what he could to ease the way to the Black population's enfranchisement.

With the help of other like-minded locals, he organized free transport to the parish seat (Convent) on Saturdays. This served the African Americans who had no way of getting there, which at the time was most of them.

Victor also put his daughters, including my mother, Helen, to work. They spent hours on his typewriter at home, creating lists of names, which Victor used to organize his approach and ensure that he reached most Black citizens eligible to vote.

A quick check on Google on the success of Earl Long's efforts shows that during his four-year term, the number of Blacks on the Louisiana voter rolls increased from 22,000 to 107,000.

*

Here's a little sidebar to that story:

At the time of the voter registration effort, Victor and Ben Rome, a wealthy bus-line operator, were feuding. Both were ardent Earl Long supporters, but Ben had more "pull" with the governor, thanks to being an important financial donor to his campaigns.

One Saturday morning, when Ben was in a mischief-making mood, he called Governor Long to inform him that Victor was *not* where he was supposed to be at that hour: On his job at the courthouse.

Aware of the feud, the governor called the courthouse, with the intention of "kicking some butt," and in so doing, return a favor to Ben. The governor asked the person who picked up the phone why Mr. Reulet was not on the job that morning.

"You're talking to him, Governor," Victor answered.

And that put an end to Rome's shady efforts to get Victor fired.

BEAUFORD PAINTS COLIN

COLIN GRAVOIS REMEMBERS BEAUFORD
by Monique Wells
December 2010

Colin Gravois has lived in Paris since 1968. He met Beauford when Beauford lived on rue Vercingétorix, and has very fond memories of him. Colin spoke at the gravesite ceremony that Les Amis held at Thiais Cemetery on October 14th. He recently recounted his memories of Beauford in an interview at his office in Antony (a suburb south of Paris).

Colin Gravois at Beauford's Graveside Commemoration Ceremony.
© Franz Fox Kennedy

Upon arriving in Paris, Colin lived for five years at the Hôtel de Blois at 50, rue Vavin, which was located very near the café Select on boulevard du Montparnasse. (The hotel was a functioning brothel when Colin lived there, with the first three floors being used for "business" and the three upper floors being reserved for long-term residents.) He recalls that the rent was only 10 francs a day – roughly $2 in those times – and that the one franc per day (20 cents) increase that the hotel proprietor charged in 1974 was considered a big deal.

Colin would often have breakfast at the café Dôme, which was only a stone's throw from his hotel. (The Dome still stands on the corner of boulevard du Montparnasse and rue Delambre.) This is where he met Beauford in 1968 or 1969. Beauford would come in at around 9 AM every day – alone – to have breakfast, and Colin became accustomed to seeing him there. He remembers being impressed by Beauford's "beatific smile." Colin said that Beauford seemed wary that people might try to take advantage of him, so at first, he did not attempt to engage Beauford in conversation about personal things.

At that time, the Dôme had a sidewalk terrace (it is enclosed today). Colin recalls that Beauford always wanted to sit in the front row, facing the street. In this way, he could watch people as they passed by. Beauford knew lots of people, so he was often quite busy greeting friends and acquaintances when he was at the Dôme.

Eventually, Colin offered to take Beauford back to his studio on rue Vercingétorix in the large black sedan (of the type used for London cabs) that he drove around town. He did this a few times before Beauford invited him up to the studio. Colin recalls that the entrance was *au fond de la cour* (at the back of the courtyard), and that it was up a flight of stairs. His most vivid

Terrace of the
Dôme Café, 1959.
Photo from
Cafés d'Artistes à Paris
(photo credit-Archives)

memory of the studio is that everything was covered with white sheets.

Colin remembers that Beauford would occasionally take meals at La Coupole, and that he also liked to eat at a restaurant called Les Mille Colonnes on rue de la Gaité. This was not very far from his studio, and it also happened to be a place where Colin and his friends invariably had dinner. Beauford would always join them if he was there. At Les Mille Colonnes you could have a full diner with wine for about $1.50. Though these prices were "Beauford's style" (affordable), Colin and his friends would chip in most of the time to take care of Beauford's bill.

By the early 1970s, Colin began to note early signs of Beauford's mental deterioration, mostly in the form of forgetfulness. Around 1973, he gave Beauford four large canvases that he had previously used for a promotional event. Beauford was grateful to receive them, and this strengthened the bond between him and Colin.

Colin's favorite memory of Beauford is of taking him for rides in his black London cab. He named the car "Bill" because the license plate began with the letters "BLL." Because the space next to the driver was reserved for luggage, Beauford always sat in the back, as a taxi passenger would. He had an excellent vantage point for viewing the city because the seat was high, and Colin remembers that Beauford would look out the window at the buildings, cars, and pedestrians with a big smile on his face.

A London Taxicab

Colin was unequivocal when he said that the most important aspects that he remembers of Beauford's persona were his kindness and gentleness — the same attributes that numerous others have cited.

Beauford painted a portrait of Colin at the Vercingétorix studio in 1974. Colin sat for Beauford a half-dozen times as the painting took shape. He remembers being seated in an armchair wearing a green army jacket. When it was almost done, Colin had his friend Kathleen photograph him with the painting, with Colin posing in the chair where he sat for the painting and the painting perched behind and above him. Kathleen also took several photographs of Beauford's studio at that time. Colin said that Beauford's signature appeared on the painting as though it had been done in pencil.

Colin then went on a trip to the U.S., thinking that he would retrieve the painting upon his return. But by the time he came back to Paris, Beauford had been taken to Saint Anne's Hospital and his studio had been vacated. Colin never saw the portrait again. He is hoping that his friend Kathleen will be able to find the photos that she took so that he will have some visual record of himself with the painting, as well as the studio.

Upon Beauford's commitment to Saint Anne's, James Baldwin most likely moved the painting to an apartment on rue des Anglais in Paris's 5th arrondissement where he stored Beauford's works and other belongings on a temporary basis. Several of these would later be shown at the Studio Museum in Harlem retrospective organized by Richard A. Long.

In looking at the catalog of that exhibition, I came across an image of a painting called Portrait of a Man in Green. Intrigued by the parallels that I noted in Colin's description of Beauford's painting of him and what I saw in the image, I contacted Colin to see if he could identify the portrait.

Portrait of a Man in Green
Beauford Delaney, Oil
(undated)
Photo from catalog of *Beauford Delaney: A Retrospective.*
Studio Museum in Harlem

155

Beauford Delaney 1953, Harlem.

Photo credit: Carl van Vechten

Both he and his daughter immediately identified Colin as the person represented there! In addition to the physical likeness (curly hair, moustache and goatee) and the armchair and green jacket, Colin said that he always wore his wristwatch on the right arm. The man in Beauford's portrait also wears his watch on the right wrist.

What a fortuitous outcome to my interview!

Monique Wells

Les Amis de Beauford Delaney

-BEAUFORD DELANEY...

In December 2010, I published an account of **Colin Gravois's** friendship with Beauford Delaney as Colin relayed it to me in an interview. Colin describes the experience of sitting for a portrait with Beauford and regretting that he

©Kathleen Modrowski

did not return to Beauford's studio to recuperate it before Beauford was committed to Saint Anne's Hospital.

Colin has managed to obtain a photograph by his friend Kathleen of him sitting in front of the portrait that Beauford created. He sent it to me to share with all of you! Here it is.

This photo was taken at Beauford's studio on rue Vercingétorix. (Note the other paintings on the wall behind Beauford's portrait of Colin.) Unlike the abstract nature of some of his portraits of James Baldwin, Beauford rendered a true likeness of Colin in this painting. Its whereabouts are currently unknown.

Monique Wells,

Les Amis de Beauford Delaney

NEEGASHOOT

All I really wanted to do growing up was hunt birds with my slingshot, although we didn't call the device by that fancy word, only our city cousins called it that. We called it a "*nee-gashoot,*" pronounced in the French manner, "NEE-ga-shoot. I have to be completely honest about that word here. It's the word the older boys used, and it was naturally passed on down to us.

The fact is, even the "colored boys" called it a neegashoot. So, I like to believe there was no mean-spirited, racist meaning in the term, that it was simply the name for a device used to sling stones at birds or small animals, or at people when we shot Chinaberry balls at each other in our war games.

The secret of a good neegashoot was twofold. First, we had to find a branch with a sufficiently strong fork to use as the base. It needed to be the right size for a small hand, not so big that it would get in the way of the projectile — usually a small, roundish rock found by the side of the road. Sometimes, if you had done well in a game of marbles, you'd pick a few of the worst-looking ones to use in your neegashoot.

Secondly, we had to find the right rubber for the slinging mechanism. This question of the quality of the rubber was a difficult one to resolve. During the War, with the rubber plantations in the Far East under Japanese control, scientists had to invent artificial rubber, which they did using petroleum-based products. That rubber was strong and reliable for industrial uses, but not for neegashoots. It didn't have the "slinging power" of natural rubber; it was just not "rubbery" enough. No. What we prized was *natural* rubber. If you could get your hands on a prewar inner tube, for example — even a portion of one (you could never find a whole one because the boys who came before you saw to that) — then you were in Neegashoot Paradise. Now you had replacement parts to last a boy's lifetime, and you also had a treasure you could parcel out to friends.

Any good hunter worth his *filé gumbo* always had a supply in the garage, because natural rubber aged faster than the ersatz variety. It could break on you at important moments, like when you were in the middle of getting off your best shot to bring down the biggest bird ever. If the rubber snapped, of course you'd miss, and that fantastic bird would get away.

When I was in about 4th grade, I received my first BB gun for Christmas, a gift from my Godmother. When the BB gun took all my attention, I stuck my neegashoot behind a rafter in the garage, never to be used again. But I still remember it well, from cutting the branch of a tree to carve it...to the way it bent a little bit backwards into my right hand instead of being completely straight, which I loved because that felt perfect to me...to attaching the rubber straps...and of course shooting it! That sense of satisfaction I got when the stone whizzed through the air and landed — smack — where I intended it to could not be equaled with a BB gun.

Newspapers, Radio, TV…

I can't recall exactly when I started reading the newspaper, but it was probably by the second grade, because I clearly remember news stories about the beginning of the Korean War, in June, 1950. With WWII a recent memory, the country did not take kindly to the idea of getting involved in another conflict. People were looking forward to getting on with their lives and sharing in the post-war prosperity that was starting to kick in. Plunging into a land war in Asia, suddenly and without warning, came as a shock to everyone, and the adults around me spoke of Korea in worried tones.

Every Sunday night when we would go "veillée" down the road at the Gravois homestead ("veillée" referred to spending an evening with family or friends), Uncle Philip, Nonc Lal (Uncle Leonard) and the other adults discussed Korea non-stop. I was there looking on, taking it all in. Both those uncles were war veterans, both quick of tongue, and each considered himself an expert on land *and* sea warfare. Nor was either shy in letting you know it. I believe even modern-day, made-for-TV pundits would have had to take a back seat to their strategizing.

Yes, indeed, Philip and Leonard put on a great show, and at the same time gave a history lesson to the little boy looking on. There was talk of "Staleen" (*Who's he?*)... Truman (who was not referred to affectionately)... The 38th Parallel (*What's that?*)... and Eisenhower, who they said should come out of retirement and wipe those Chinese off the map (*What map?*). MacArthur was also mentioned, and favorably, having been Nonc Lal's overall commander in the late war.

"Je te dis, Philippe, MacArthur va clean out tout ça si Truman le lache!"

("I'm telling you, Phillippe, MacArthur will clean them out if Truman lets him loose!")

Actually, Truman did *let him loose* before a year was out but in a different way.

I followed all that in the *New Orleans States-Item*, an afternoon paper Daddy brought home every night. It was not delivered in the area of town where we lived, so the paperboy dropped it at my father's shop in Front Vacherie. Every night when he got home from work, he'd get out of his truck with the paper under his arm, bring it inside and put it on the table for us. (He read it later in bed.)

Daddy usually got home from work around five o'clock. During the summer months when the days were longer, we often had some chores to do in the yard. But at the other times of the year, we sat down to supper as soon as he arrived, and after eating, the newspaper and the radio served as our entertainment.

One program we would listen to without fail was the CBS evening news on WWL — a clear channel station in New Orleans, "870 on your dial."

The news was delivered by none other than the most celebrated of radio newscasters: Edward R. Morrow. All the adults knew him because he had reported from England for CBS during the war. Murrow brought the war home to America with his daily broadcast: "This...is London," assisted by his team of "Morrow boys" from around Europe. At the time I was listening to him, he had a 15-minute nightly news program broadcast from New York. It came on at 6 o'clock, and after about 13 minutes or so, he'd pause for a commercial break, saying, "I'll be back in a moment...with the word for tomorrow" in that beautiful, resonant voice of his. After a minute of commercials, he'd come back with some little gem of suspense or nugget of wisdom to hold us until the next day.

Murrow closed each show with his famous signoff: "Good night, and good luck," which became the title of the film George Clooney made about him a few years ago. He had a voice made for radio — personable, powerful, authoritative. And he was a wonderful newsman, too, inspiring me (as did my grandfather) to take an interest in the events of the day, whether national or global.

After the news, we often continued to listen to the radio, depending on what was on or how much homework was left to do. This was during the period later referred to as, "The Golden Age of Radio." Several programs that we listened to faithfully were detective shows that kept us riveted in deep suspense from night to night. "Mr. & Mrs. North." "The Squeaking Door" (and the sound of that door squeaking at the beginning of each show sent shivers up my spine!) "Mr. Keen, Tracer of Lost Persons." And "Johnny Dollar, Insurance Investigator."

Funny how we always looked at the radio while we listened. We could have heard it from another room or been in the same room facing another direction, but no, we had to face the radio. Almost as if it were a human being talking directly to us, and we had to *see* it's face in order to understand fully what was being said. The programs were well put together and kept you on the edge of your seat. It's difficult to explain to people brought up on television how entertaining radio was in those days, how important a part it played in peoples' lives, how just plain down-to-earth *good* it was. I *still* love radio!

And then came...television. The death knell of radio and the beginning of a new era. For us, television marked the end of summer evenings on the front porch.

I saw my first television set in the "grand metropolis" of Bayou Boeuf, a fishing village deep in the woods. One night after work — it must have been in late 1949 — Daddy came home and picked us up, saying we had an errand to run. The "errand," it turned out, was that he had heard there was a television set in Bayou Boeuf, and he wanted to see it. We took the half-hour's drive from our house to a bar, now called Larousse's, where the television was said to be located.

The place was unusually quiet inside. A crowd of people standing around, everyone looking towards the left side of the room — not the typical, after-work barroom scene. I wiggled my way to the front of the throng. At the end of the counter there was a little contraption with black and white images dancing around inside it, and with sound, too, like a radio. It had a small screen, only about 6 by 8 inches. But to increase the size of the image, there was a large square magnifying glass positioned about 10 inches from the screen, so if you looked at the television front and center through that device, the picture almost doubled in size.

Before TV, we'd spend several evenings a week on one of two large front porches — Pépère's or Aunt Marie's. Some of us enjoyed sitting in the four or five old-time rockers, some in chairs, some on the floor with legs dangling over the edge. Talk was about everything and nothing, watching the cars pass by, heads moving side to side with each automobile, like spectators at a tennis match, commenting on each one.

"Hey! You saw Tee-Beb's got a new Ford? Wonder what kind of deal Cazenave gave him to junk that old Chevrolet..."

"See how close she was sitting to him? Better not tell her daddy about *that!*"

"Looks like Bobotte bought a "new" jalopy. Wonder how far this one's going to take him?"

"I see Ikay has a new load of watermelons. Doubt if they're gonna be as sweet as that last batch he got in Alabama."

And on and on until the mosquitoes ran us back home.

*

Pépère Victor bought his first television set some months after WDSU started broadcasting from New Orleans. Now, his was a bigger one than the one we saw in Bayou Boeuf; I reckon the screen was about 18 inches on the diagonal, impressive for the time. Pépère was the only person in our neighborhood who owned a TV, too, so the acquisition was a major event in our lives. I couldn't help noticing that Pépère and Mémère acquired quite a number of new friends after that purchase!

But from then on, after television arrived, we spent our evenings indoors in the dark, eyes riveted to the bright screen.

And that was the end of conversation in Vacherie as we knew it.

Pépère's front porch where we spent many evenings before television.

ANTOINE, EXCEPTIONAL GARDENER

Who would imagine that the majestic pecan tree was domesticated in Vacherie, Louisiana? It never crossed our minds — we who grew up in the shade of the three biggest pecan trees in the region, and maybe the world. And it wasn't until we were older that we took note of the fact that it was a slave — Antoine, from the Beau Séjour Plantation — who played a decisive role in the domestication of the pecan.

In the winter of 1846, Jacques Télesphore Roman, the owner of Beau Séjour, invited Dr. A. E. Colomb of New Orleans, whose efforts to produce a superior variety of pecan through grafting had not yet succeeded, to conduct further experiments at his plantation.

For years, Dr. Colomb had been trying to develop a high-quality pecan cultivar. Up to that time, pecans were collected from trees found in the wild, but from tree to tree the quality and size varied, which meant that the fruits of the wild trees had no real commercial viability.

Beau Séjour Plantation (today Oak Alley) was an ideal place for Colomb to continue his experiments. Firstly, there was a lot of land to plant trees on, and secondly, Roman's slave, Antoine, had outstanding abilities as a gardener.

Dr. Colomb came to Beau Séjour with cuttings from a superior tree he'd found on Anita Plantation across the Mississippi, a tree which produced the most excellent pecans he'd ever seen. By grafting the cuttings, he hoped to develop a hardy, high-quality pecan, suitable for commercial purposes. Antoine was a talented apprentice who quickly succeeded in grafting 16 trees. In time, he grafted 110 trees — a whole orchard — situated toward the back of the property. By 1865 they had achieved maturity and were bearing excellent quality pecans.

In 1876, pecans from the Vacherie trees were exhibited at the Centennial Exposition in Philadelphia. They were so well received that they were awarded a certificate in which the variety was commended for its "remarkably large size, tenderness of shell, and very special excellence." The name, Centennial, was chosen for this variety, to honor the 100th anniversary of the birth of the nation.

Unfortunately, however, Beau Séjour changed hands in the economic turbulence after the Civil War, and despite the fact that the nuts were bringing high prices, the new owners cleared out a large number of those magnificent trees to make way for the more-profitable sugar cane, and the Vacherie pecan project faded into oblivion.

From the Smithsonian: *J.T. Roman's notations regarding Antoine state only that he was "a Creole Negro gardener and expert grafter of pecan trees." But Antoine, like so many enslaved individuals hidden from the world, was much more. His skill ultimately made possible the propagation of more than 1,000 different pecan varieties, which today are planted commercially in 14 states and on every continent except Antarctica. Our na-*

tion's history of slavery cannot be glossed over — but within that tragedy are countless examples of courage, perseverance, and contribution which have made America what it is today. Antoine's story is one of these.

Centennial pecans, shelled and just waiting
to make fudge or pralines.

BLACK STORIES

(Part II)

Strange Ballet

Black people had to sometimes go through crazy contortions to accommodate themselves to segregation. An African American friend from Vacherie, Lawrence Keller, told me the following story as an example of the kind of experience that was an everyday reality for him.

As a young man, Loonie, as Lawrence is called by his friends, worked for my uncle Philip Becnel at his grocery store in Front Vacherie. He delivered groceries, stacked shelves, and fulfilled the role of general roustabout around the store.

Once a week, he and Philip's brother-in-law and partner, Leonard, went by truck to New Orleans to get supplies.

They normally made five or six stops around the city, the main one being at a large warehouse on Tchoupitoulas Street.

To be neighborly, they sometimes gave a ride to people in the area who had business in the city but no way to get there. Once, they took a woman (I'll call her

Rita) who needed to get to Charity Hospital to see one of her small children, who was receiving long-term care.

During the ride to the city, everyone was in a friendly, joking mood. Leonard drove and the woman sat between the two men. Loonie said she took a lively part in the conversation, and during the trip, everything was "copacetic."

When they arrived at the warehouse, Loonie's first task was to accompany Rita on public transport to Charity Hospital. She didn't know the city and was afraid to make her way to the hospital alone. That's when the racial ballet kicked in. Rita could not be seen traveling with Loonie; White people

Uncles Philip and Leonard's country general store where Loonie was employed.

might think she had Black friends, and that was unacceptable. So, she would walk about 10 feet behind him all the way to the bus stop.

At the bus stop, they stood waiting at an acceptable distance from each other, never once looking at the other openly.

When they boarded the bus, Loonie was of course relegated to the section in the back.

As they approached their final stop, Loonie walked up to the front of the bus, which indicated to Rita that they would be getting off next.

After they disembarked, she followed him to Charity Hospital, all the while walking 10 paces behind. Never once did either of them acknowledge knowing the other. Loonie walked up to the White entrance of the hospital, which signaled her where to enter, then pretended to have made a mistake. He turned around and went back to the warehouse to help load the truck.

In mid-afternoon, he took the bus back to Charity Hospital to collect Rita, and they went through the same complicated charade on their way back to the warehouse. Never once during the trip to and from Charity Hospital could he allow himself to address her or indicate in any way that he knew her.

This is one small illustration of how African-Americans had to accommodate themselves to segregation on a daily basis, if they wanted to survive. Sad but true.

Passing: A Peculiar Way of Life

I think it's fair to say that for most African Americans in the days of my youth in the Deep South, crossing the color line was more a matter of survival than of cultural identity.

For some people, passing opens the door to a better chance of succeeding in a White-dominated society. For others, to "pass" is to sin against one's authenticity. But the problem is that you could never go back. Once you passed for a White person (by virtue of having very light skin and adopting white peoples' mores and manners so impeccably that you fit seamlessly into their lives), your new family and friends thought of you as *one of them* — even though you knew that you were playing a role. Fooling people. Not what you said you were. Not *one of them.*

But neither could you turn around and invite your White friends into your former community of "colored people." This is why it's easy to imagine how passing could create intense inner turmoil in a person. But the brutal reality remained: those who had more opportunities for achieving a better life. So regardless of the psychological discomforts of passing, many a light-skinned Black person tried to get ahead in the world by doing so.

A close friend of mine, E.J. Gilbert, Jr. of New Orleans, grew up straddling the color line; both his parents were considered "white enough," meaning they actually looked White. His father passed so well, in fact, that he was able to work as a master electrician on ships, at a time when Blacks were limited to holding menial jobs like cooking, serving, and hard labor. But when the boats docked at home in New Orleans, Mr. Gilbert Sr. returned to his Black family.

E.J. lived in a mixed neighborhood, so it wasn't unusual to see White people around. "I was never angry, like some folks, about someone in their family passing," he told me, "because my father took care of us that way. I understood that he had to go that route to put food on our table and give us a better life. No big deal."

E.J. Gilbert, Jr, New Orleans 2010.

He tells a story about one incident when he had to protect his mother's identity. On streetcars and buses in the days of segregation in New Orleans, there was a wooden bar that fit into the back of a seat, on which was written: For Colored Only. Blacks were obliged by law to sit behind that sign. When a White person got on a bus, if there were no empty seats in the front, he would just pick up the sign and move it back one row. Any Black person occupying a seat that was now suddenly in the "White Section" had to get up and move farther back, in order to allow the White person to sit.

Once when he was a young boy, E.J. caught the bus going from downtown to the St. Bernard area, where he was living. When he boarded, he saw his mother sitting in the front, White section. Well, he says, he had enough sense to know that if he sat next to her, or even acknowledged that he knew her, she would have to get up and go to the back with him. So, he just smiled at her, winked, and went to sit in the back of the bus.

His Aunt Louise's husband, Eddie, passed for White, too. He worked at Picou's Bakery, E.J.s favorite place. White kids, Black kids...everybody went to Picout's. But when E.J. went to the bakery, he couldn't just say, "Hey, Uncle Eddie." All he could do was order his doughnuts. Maybe, if he bought a dozen, Eddie might put 14 in the bag, but it could not be known that they were family. Eddie could have lost his job had his boss known he was actually Black.

E.J. recalls, "When I was on my bicycle riding down the street with my White friends, and saw Eddie walking to work, I didn't holler, 'Hi, Uncle Eddie!' I had that much sense! Didn't want those White kids knowing that Eddie was passing. Passing was our means of survival. But it was also something I respected him for. No matter what people said, Eddie found a way to take care of his family — and that way was working White. If passing was the ticket to be able to keep his family alive and well, I respected him for doing it."

Even more convoluted is the story of his Aunt Blanche. She was married to a Black man who passed for White, and their children passed, too. Two daughters married White men from Mississippi. When Blanche died, they were obliged to have two funerals because her daughters couldn't go to a Black funeral home with their White husbands. So, E.J.s side, the Black side, held her wake in one funeral home, and the next day they moved the body to a White funeral home and held a second wake there for the White relatives from Mississippi. After the two wakes, Charbonnay, a Black mortuary, buried Blanche. "That was the way it had to be done," E.J. says, "crazy stuff. But we had to work around the system."

Blanche regularly warned her daughters, "You've got to stop making babies. You keep making these babies, somewhere along the way one is going to come out Black!"

One of the daughters gave birth to a lot of kids, and sure enough, her sixth baby came out, "...almost darkish red." said E.J. "With Brillo-type hair."

Her husband never accused her of fooling around with a Black man, though. No. He accused her of fooling around with a *Jew!* That was the best he could come up with to account for the baby's appearance. And it was a way he could save face as a White man in Mississippi. People believing your wife slept with a dark-skinned, wiry-haired Sephardic Jew wasn't ideal. But it was a lot "better" than letting them think she slept with an African-American.

"Now ain't that some crazy stuff?" E.J. asked rhetorically, shaking his head.

Rudi Lombard, Donna Dorsey Gilbert, E.J. Gilbert, Jr.,
New Orleans 2010.

Underage Activist

A short excerpt from Rudi Lombard's 2014 obituary in the New Orleans Times Picayune: *"Lombard led a sit-in at a segregated lunch counter on Canal Street in New Orleans. He and four others were arrested. The case which bears his name, Lombard v. Louisiana, went all the way to the U.S. Supreme Court. The high court overturned the arrests, and the case was one of several that became precedents for striking down segregation laws and practices."*

Rudi Lombard grew up in Algiers, a part of New Orleans on the West Bank of the Mississippi. His mother was a domestic who cooked and cleaned for White people, and his father was a hospital orderly.

When Rudi was coming up, he lived in an integrated neighborhood; New Orleans was not significantly residentially segregated at the time. But after the civil rights movement got underway, the city's housing areas became more and more separate.

Rudi's mother worked for a White man, the president of the New Orleans Cotton Exchange, in his mansion on Napoleon Avenue, uptown. As a child, when Rudi accompanied his mother to work, he was not allowed to enter the big house, but had to remain outside in the yard or in the carriage house where the chauffer, Henry, lived.

"Well, it's funny," Rudi recalls, "it seems I always knew why I wasn't allowed inside — no one had to tell me. I always *knew*. Yeah...I was born knowing. *[laughs]*. I don't remember a time when I didn't *know*. I grew up with a consciousness informed by the circumstances in which we lived, from Day One. We always knew there was a place for Blacks and a place for Whites. We played with White kids on the street and in the back yards, but we didn't go into their houses. We were never invited inside."

Whites started moving out of Rudi's neighborhood in large numbers in the 1960s. By the time he got to elementary school, relationships between the races had begun to deteriorate. White kids went off to the White schools and Rudi went to a Black, Catholic school.

"I grew up Baptist first," he told me, "then my mother and I converted to Catholicism in order for me to be able to go to a better elementary school, a parochial school. My parents thought I would receive a better education there than at the public school. And I'm sure that was correct."

It was in that school that Rudi had his first important shift in consciousness, inspired by conversations with a White priest, Father Brown, originally from Baltimore. Brown was assigned to All Saints parish when Rudi was in seventh grade. Father Brown had a kind disposition and had difficulty accepting the segregation he encountered in New Orleans. In his conversations with Rudi, he expressed frustration and distress with the system. Segregation in church was especially offensive to him — "In God's house!" he used to say. This was the first time Rudi had ever encountered a White adult who articulated a sense of moral outrage at the injustice — the sheer *wrongness* — of segregation.

Rudi organized his first public protest against segregation when he was still in grade school. During recess, the White kids played in a park near the school while the Black kids were limited to playing on the apron of the park — a three-  yard-wide section of ground between the fence that separated the two playing areas and the street. Father Brown repeatedly expressed his disapproval of that situation.

"I remember thinking: *He's having a tough time with this thing.* And I didn't like it either. Yeah, he was a White man...who expressed disdain for that divided playground. I had never heard any other White person express concern about it before. He was the first White I ever heard say, 'Something's wrong with this. This is not right!' So, I'm thinking, *This man is interesting!* Because when you grow up the way I grew up, you knew that Whites would do anything — *anything* — I mean to the point of taking your life if necessary — to maintain the status quo and preserve segregation."

One day at recess, Rudi was pitching a football with a pal and he decided to throw it into the White playground. Intentionally.

"I just threw it in the park. Don't know what came over me. My pal Larry said, 'You crazy?' I said, 'No.'"

Rudi crawled under the fence to retrieve the ball, and Larry called, "What you doing now?"

He expected Rudi to throw the ball back to the other side, but Rudi said, "You want to play Pitch with me, Larry, you've got to come in *here*."

Larry answered, "N......! You *crazy?*"

And again, Rudi answered, "No." Then he baited his friend, "If you want to play with me with this ball, you've got to *come in here*."

After Rudi refused to get out of the White kids' park, Larry crawled under the fence to join him. The two young friends then started to play pitch and catch in the forbidden zone.

"Then the Black kids came over to that fence to look at us," Rudi told me, laughing, "They were shocked and said, 'What's wrong with those two? They lost their minds?'"

But before long, the Black kids crawled under the fence and started playing on the White side. People from the neighborhood came out in throngs to see what was going on. Black and White — everyone came over to gawk. But the Black kids continued to play in the "off limits" area right up until the bell rang.

By this time, the whole neighborhood was in an uproar, and that's when the cops showed up. They drove around, looking at the situation, asking questions.

Finally, the pupils went back to their classrooms. The cops marched into the school and demanded, "Who started this?"

But the nuns wouldn't talk.

School was dismissed at three o'clock and Rudi went home. His father worked from eleven at night to seven in the morning, and was in bed resting. But when Rudi went to his room, he saw a case of *Barq's Root Beer* at the foot of his bed. It turned out that his father had heard what Rudi had done — by that time everybody in the neighborhood except the cops knew what had happened — and this was his way of praising Rudi and telling him he was a hero that day.

"My dad knew how much I loved root beer." Rudi recalls, looking back wistfully at that day in his life. "I don't like it anymore, but back then *Barq's* was the favorite for people like me. That was my first civil rights protest. And it informed my consciousness on segregation. Just never forgot that day."

UNFORGETTABLES

The Mad Stone of Vacherie

In folk medicine, a "mad stone" is a special device used to treat snake and spider bites. We had a "mad stone" at my Gravois grandparents' home in Vacherie.

The story goes that my great-grandparents came into possession of the stone after taking in an Indian who was gravely ill and nursing him back to health. He was one of the few remaining native Americans in our area; most of the tribes had relocated by then.

The Indian returned to the house sometime later and gave Great-Pépère and Great-Mémère the stone as a gesture of thanks. It was said to have come from the heart of a deer — a detail which may be apocryphal; history is silent on the matter.

I don't know where the stone got the appellation "mad." We just called it, "the stone" or "*la pierre.*" It probably acquired that descriptive from an article published in the New Orleans *Times-Picayune*, in 1947, the title of which was, *The Mad Stone of Vacherie* (see below).

A "mad stone" is not a stone at all, in fact. It's a porous material found in the digestive track of animals and, some claim, in the heart. Being porous, it was believed to draw the poison from infections. The stone would actually cling to the wound, and if, for example, the bite was on your hand and you placed the stone on it then turned your hand over, it would hold fast and not fall off. When the poison was all drawn out, the stone would release itself naturally, like a leech who's had his fill of blood.

Since grandmother Berthe's death in 1959, *la pierre* has held an honored place in the home of her daughter, Aunt Therese, who continued to administer treatment with it. But nowadays, with the advent of antibiotics and modern medicine "business has gone down," one could say, and people seldom come to Vacherie seeking a cure for poisonous animal bites.

In the 1940s and '50s, when we went visiting at our grandparents, we'd sometimes find strangers in the house, with Mémère giving them treatment — "*traîtement avec la pierre*." First Mémère would prick the wound with a needle she had sterilized in the flame of a match, then she'd apply the stone. Depending on the venomousness of the poison, people would spend from a few hours to several days, waiting for the stone to do its job. It was a well-known treatment at the time, and people came from all over south Louisiana to receive it. There was no fixed charge; patients just gave what they could.

After the original stone fell and broke into several pieces, Mémère used those smaller bits with the same success she'd had with the whole. She kept them in a round metal box stuffed with cotton, that bore the unlikely label: *Indian Ointment*.

Theories on the stone's effectiveness or non-effectiveness are legion. But the essential point is: it seemed to work a lot of the time.

Now, as to the question of whether mad stones cured people through some chemical interaction with their body, or through their power as a panacea, we're still waiting for the allopathic professionals to weigh in on that.

The New Orleans Times Picayune of June 19, 1949, featured a story and pictures of my grandparents Ernest Gravois and his wife, Berthe Rodrigue, the Mad Stone, and their family home in Vacherie.

"There is nothing unusual about the home of Ernest G. Gravois, Box 200, Vacherie, La. It sits off the Back Vacherie road on a green lawn clipped close by grazing cows and a plodding horse. Its weathered boards and its picket fence look like any other of a dozen houses along the oyster-shell road. But the house of Ernest Gravois is perhaps the best-known structure in the entire Vacherie area. It is the house of the 'Mad Stone of Vacherie.'"

"Come back to some 150 years ago when only two White families struggled against the forests and floods of that rugged country, when Indians and their mystic methods, customs and tribal remedies were the 'law of the prophets' thereabouts. The

Gravois and the Webre families were the sturdy pioneers, Louisiana style, who began hacking out a farm back from the river. The Indians were friendly, especially a neighboring tribe which lived on the shores what is today called Lake Des Allemands."

"One day Madame Gravois went to her vegetable garden for a cabbage. Suddenly, she jumped back in fright as a deadly snake struck at her hand. Two telltale fang pricks, and the serpent was gone. Mme. Gravois ran into the log cabin house, calling for her husband. The hand began to swell. The Webres and the Gravoises made her as comfortable as they could, but she grew steadily worse."

"Suddenly, into the small clearing around the house, walked an Indian clutching a small piece of black stone. In sign language, he indicated that if they would take him to the woman, he would cure her. Inside the cabin they watched as the native applied the small stone to the marks left by the snake's fangs. The stone remained there as if securely fastened. Seconds passed, minutes, hours. All sat as if hypnotized. Finally, Mme. Gravois' eyes opened. She became noticeably better. At last she sat up. The stone fell from her hand. The Indian picked it up, asked for clear water in a basin and dropped the stone gently into it. It bubbled for a minute. Then he removed it and departed."

"So, the legend goes, Mme. Gravois' cure was complete. The story continues one year later. This time the Indian came down with a malady, some kind of internal illness not connected with a snake or animal bite, evidently. Now it was the turn of the French people to help him. The cure was not so quick. He remained with the Gravoises and the Webres for a long period until he was well. Before departing however, he gave them as a token of his gratitude the shiny, black stone, about 3 inches long, as big around as a man's thumb, they say. He told them to keep it as a treasure, never to sell it. It would always work for them and theirs."

* * * * *

Here's what one Mad Stone user wrote about his experience:
"A few years ago while at work, I was bitten under my right arm by a black widow spider. Being the 'not sick enough for the doctor' and as the old people say 'it'll pass' attitude, I headed to North Louisiana for the weekend. On the way home, I developed a streak down my arm and a slight fever. It was a Sunday and no doctors were open. I had heard the legend of the Mad Stone all my life. I quickly realized that was the chance to finally see and actually watch the Mad Stone at work. I went to see Therese Gravois Oubre, the stone's caretaker. She pricked the bite, applied the stone, and it stuck for almost an hour and a half. You could feel the tiny, almost vacuum suction. She washed the small stone and it actually bubbled as if it were slightly boiling. The next day, work sent me to the doctor to have the bite checked out. The doctor said that there was nothing he could do since it seemed that the bite had drained and left no infection whatsoever."

Nightmare in Priestly Garb

It was a cool and crisp Sunday morning in October, 1949, a time of year when sugarcane harvesting was in full swing, and the sugar houses were grinding around the clock. At our church, Notre Dame de la Paix, a priest walked tentatively out of the sacristy and took his place at the altar. He nodded to the two altar boys waiting for him and began preparations for Mass.

I was in church that morning with Mama, Daddy, Mémère, and Lael, seated in pew N° 8 on the right side — the Reulet family's regular place. (Pews were rented annually back then.)

As the priest began to utter a few words in Latin, a perceptible buzz could be heard all over the church. People were startled. They began to whisper, and even talked out loud, looking over their shoulders toward the entrance of the church, as if expecting someone to walk in and put a stop to this funny business...

Then the stranger at the altar turned to the congregation and said in a friendly voice, "Good morning. I'm Father Daniel Becnel, I'm your new priest." And he spoke in English. In ENGLISH!

Looks of incredulity swept over the faces of the congregants. This wasn't their usual priest. This new man had a kind face and a warm voice...had God in Heaven finally heard their calls of distress? Were years of prayers being answered at last?

Whether or not this was a case of Divine Intervention, one thing was certain: their long nightmare was over at last. Because it is no exaggeration to say that for more than a quarter century, the townspeople of our small, French-speaking town in south Louisiana were held hostage by a cruel oppressor. A sadist and tormentor. I refer, sadly, to our parish priest Père (Father) Augustin Delnom. The man who was, for the first time in 28 years, *not* standing at the altar that blessed Sunday.

Père Augustin Delnom, around 1935.

Delnom was from France and was sent to Vacherie in 1921 by the Archdiocese of New Orleans, to minister to the spiritual needs of the community. People said he acted so crazy because he had been gassed in WWI. They needed to justify his behavior somehow...to believe it wasn't really his fault that he was such a monster. Believing an abuser can't help himself makes it easier for the victims to endure his travesties.

His story is little known outside the area where it took place. People who were alive during his reign of terror want to forget what happened, and those who came after know only a few strands of the story. Even after more than 70 years, many are still hesitant to talk about it. There is a pall that can linger over people who have been mistreated — a cloud of shame, as if they believe they are at fault themselves for the traumas imposed on them. This is particularly true of children who trust that adults are always in the right. And then, of course, there is also the simple human desire to try to steer clear of memories that make us suffer. Whatever the case, to say the people of Vacherie were oppressed does not begin to do justice to the woe they endured. The word doesn't capture the wrecking of minds and souls that one man perpetrated. Nor does it capture the horror of the bodily harm he inflicted.

Augustin Delnom. A despot beholden to no one. A priest who terrorized the inhabitants of our little town. And no one knew how to stop him. He ran roughshod over everyone — bullied them into submission. Over and over. And seemingly without fear of retribution or legal process, for he set himself up as The Law unto himself, and no one questioned him. Every despicable thing he said or did, he claimed to do *in the name of God*. It was as if the devil had disguised himself as a priest and gotten a grip on our sleepy little backwater settlement...but now things were being set right — *he was gone!*

After Mass that bright Sunday, people gathered in front of the church, everyone so excited it was like Easter and Christmas rolled into one. They didn't walk straight to their cars like they would on an ordinary Sunday. Everyone wanted to kiss and hug each other. They needed to celebrate! For decades the people of Vacherie had forgotten what a civilized and tranquil thing a Sunday service could be. Now they could start living their lives with a sense of safety again. A sense of normalcy. The prison gate had finally flung open and the relief — the joy — was irrepressible.

For weeks after, people shared their stories of Delnom. No one could speak of much else! Truth is: we *still* talk about him. We still commiserate — over 70 years later.

The very day that Delnom left Vacherie (October 22, 1949), he had two funeral services to perform. The first was for Pépère Ernest Gravois, Daddy's father, who died at 86 in his own bed, after a long and full life. Then he presided over afternoon services for Aunt Constantine Reulet, Pépère Victor's sister, who had committed suicide in the early hours before dawn, hanging herself in a mule stall in the barn behind Aunt Marie's house.

Delnom carried out these two priestly duties in his usual severe and humorless manner, making no allusions to his pending departure for later that evening. He left like "*un voleur dans la nuit*" (a thief in the night), as people used to describe such furtive departures.

For many months after he left, it was rare for a conversation between adults not to swing back to Père Delnom.

They talked about the time Jourdan Falgoust confronted Delnom with a pistol in church...about the time Delnom smacked little Albert Gravois around then locked him in his chicken coop as punishment for "misbehaving" at catechism. (Delnom had asked: "When did Jesus Christ die?" and Albert answered, "I didn't even know he was sick.")

People talked of the times when Delnom stopped his car to give someone a good shaking because the "sinner" had not recognized him with enough deference when he passed. This happened too many times to count, thanks to that wrecked man's overpowering need to be acknowledged by others. Then there were the times (oh, how many.) when he'd pull a person out of the confessional, give him a few smacks, then start shouting judgments and threats like a mad man — instead of offering the guilt-ridden soul compassion and forgiveness. In one such moment of uncontrolled rage, he pulled cousin Dick Reulet out of the confessional and almost pulled his ears off.

There seemed to be only one hero in the Delnom saga, only one person who ever dared to hold him accountable: the brave Eutrope Folse. He waited for the priest after Mass one Sunday and nailed him for something he'd said from the pulpit. As far as I know, this was the only moment in nearly 30 years where anyone dared to stand up in public to Augustin Delnom.

Delnom arrived in Vacherie with a woman in tow, Victoire, a French lady who remained with him throughout his tenure and left with him on the day of his departure. They were a team. At first, no one speculated out loud what her duties were, besides serving as Delnom's maid and cook. But the longer she stayed, the more tongues wagged.

They both came from solid French country stock, so farm tasks were not alien to them. Throughout their long stay in Vacherie, they raised cattle for meat and milk; kept a large vegetable garden; made cheeses; raised chickens, hogs and other farm animals, and kept bees for honey — just like any other farm couple in our part of the world. Once or twice a month, Delnom would go to the French Market in New Orleans to sell some of his produce, honey or some other thing from the church farm that could bring in some cash to supplement his $100 monthly salary.

*

For all the fear Delnom instilled in people, he also spawned a fun game called "Playing Père Delnom" in which his insanity was theatricalized by the locals. I frequently went to see a version of the show, performed just up the road by a gang of boys seven or eight years older than me, who hung around cousin Dick's house. This was how we had a rousing good time on many a rainy day in summer.

The format of the game was simple: someone was designated to play Père Delnom and the others played his victims. The skit could be set in catechism, at Sunday service, on the road — or anywhere else where Delnom had caused a stir. But whatever the setting, the main rule was that the person playing Delnom should act as crazy as the real one. He could curse the other kids, insult their mothers, hit them, kick them, pull their ears — in short, no holds barred.

The Delnom impersonator usually wielded a small aluminum pot with a handle — the kind used for boiling water for coffee. It was lightweight, and very thin, and all battered up.

That meant it didn't do much damage when someone got whacked on the head. Sometimes fights did break out, however, when the "whackee" felt the boy playing Delnom was acting *too much* like the real thing. Generally, though, the shows were a source of laughter and relief — a therapeutic rebalancing of the actual situation. A way of taking power back into our own hands by laughing at Evil.

Many if not most of the sketches were based on what happened in catechism class. My friend Elton Oubre told a story of one particular Saturday morning:

That day, Father Delnom got to asking his favorite theological question yet again: "Who killed Jesus Christ?"

The six boys in the first pew answered, each one in turn, "The Jews." That's what Delnom had taught them was the correct answer. But even if last Saturday it had been correct, this Saturday each boy got pulled out of his pew, dragged into the side aisle, spit on, forced to his knees, slapped on both ears, and knocked down flat on the floor with a good one to the back of the head.

Second pew: same question, same answers, same punishment.

Once in a while a boy would try a different answer, like: "The Germans" or "The Romans." But whatever he dared to say, he got the same brutal treatment as the others.

The result was that pretty soon we had 12 beat-up boys kneeling in the aisle whimpering, while the rest of the class looked on in terror.

Then to the third row: Who killed Jesus Christ? Ellis Falgoust stuttered, "Da...da...da...da...da...JAPS!"

I pictured him getting slaughtered like all the other sacrificial lambs before him, but Father Delnom shocked me by saying, That was a good answer. He then dismissed the trampled boys so they could return to their places.

Delnom's capriciousness, his illogical changeability, was as terrifying as his violence because of course, without consistency, we didn't know where we stood. Anything could happen at any moment — and that put us in an anxious state of constant Red Alert. So much so that when we saw his car coming in the distance, we ran and hid.

*

Stories of unstable men who abuse power and impose perverse desires on children are legion today. The ugly truths are crawling out into the sunlight at last — especially in the United States — and a social revolution is in process to make the people who behave in such ways accountable, morally and legally. But in the days of Père Delnom, the traumas perpetrated by priests were kept secret — not only by church authorities, but by the victims themselves. This is partly because people believed that the role of *priest* was a guarantee of a man's holiness...his higher knowledge...his closeness to God. We mistook the role he played for the character of the man. Truth is: we can find more *holiness* in a wino on the street, a pecan tree in full bloom, or a busy little possum. Yes, indeed... a possum is a holy thing. While many a priest is NOT.

RAWS MAH GONNE

The passing of Emerante Inness Triche some time ago brought back vivid memories of her mother, Rose McGowan Inness Simon, a not-too-distant neighbor of ours. Rose was my mother's Godmother. Her name was pronounced the French way, sounding like the English word "raws," and she was always referred to by her full name, Rose McGowan, spoken rapidly as one word, "Raws-Mah-Gonne."

Rose came to Vacherie as an orphan from the New York Home for Foundlings, and was adopted by a middle-aged, unmarried woman, Euphemie Falgoust.

Euphemie (or "cousine Mimi") was the sister of two of the wealthiest men in Vacherie. This is why, after Rose came into her inheritance, she could afford a brand-new luxury De Soto or Continental every year, and could take trips to Mexico and California. Her daughter, Betty Jane, recounted details of the trips to us neighborhood kids after they returned. Those romantic stories set us all to dreaming...Of palm trees swaying...White sails against the blue Pacific...Surfers balancing on silver waves...Tanned ladies in bright-colored bathing suits lounging on stretches of white sand...Happy people, eating ocean catch and sipping tropical fruit drinks...shimmering images of things that seemed so magical and far away, they would surely always remain beyond our reach.

*

So, anyway, Rose came to Vacherie as a young girl in inauspicious circumstances. At the time (early 1900's), potential parents could actually *place an order* for "The type of child you want to adopt." Euphemie specified that she wanted a girl with blue eyes and dark hair.

The children came down from New York by *Orphan Train* and were dropped off along the way with their adoptive parents — a practice that lasted until the late 1920s.

When her train arrived at the Vacherie depot, little Rose — a four-year-old with blue eyes and dark hair — was warmly welcomed by Euphemie and other members of her family. Although she spoke no French and Euphemie knew little English, they took readily to each other. It was a few days later when her new mother washed Rose's hair that the color ran. Euphemie saw that Rose was a *strawberry blonde!* But Euphemie kept the girl as her own, regardless of being tricked by the orphanage about her appearance, and Rose went on to have a very colorful life in Vacherie.

*

When she was older, Rose was at her doctor's office in Thibodaux one day when a woman in the waiting room remarked that she looked exactly like a friend of hers; perhaps they were sisters? Rose said that wasn't possible because she came from New York originally, had been adopted, and her name was McGowan. The woman said her friend was also from New

York, also adopted and also named McGowan. And she had even come down to Louisiana on an *Orphan Train* about the same time Rose did.

They arranged a meeting, and it turned out that the two strangers did resemble each other. They became friends and always referred to themselves as sisters, but they could never get definite proof of having a blood relationship, as adoption records were sealed then as now, and DNA identification was a thing of the future.

Rose developed a bit of a reputation as an eccentric over the course of her life, and broke the social codes of the day by divorcing her first husband, Mack Inness. She always had a stern demeanor; I never knew her to smile. She was one person not to be trifled with.

Her second husband, Melvin Simon, 14 years her junior, had a grocery store and bar not far from our house. Sometimes, if I went by early in the morning when no one was around, and if she was in a good mood, Rose would give me a little something or other. One time, she gave me one of those new ballpoint pens with a retractable point — a fascinating invention, considered to be the *ne plus ultra* of writing instruments at the time. I had a lot of envious friends at school until the day I lost it.

*

In the early 1950s, the first business place in Vacherie to have air-conditioning was Rose McGowan's grocery and bar, near the Tri-Corner service station. Rose owned the place, of course, but it was called Yompay's — after her husband's nickname.

Air conditioning was then in its infancy. On the outside of Yompay's was a colossal cooling unit, a wooden tower about 5 x 5 feet square, and taller than the building itself. That huge structure had wooden slats on the upper part, and circulating water was sent cascading down on the slats, losing heat in the process. The water fell into the refrigerated area below to be re-cooled before being circulated again in the store. It was a strange contraption, but it chilled the place wonderfully. Nowadays, every house in the US has air conditioning, and Youmpay's humongous cooling contraption has been miniaturized to the size of a 3-foot square, by 2-foot high refrigerating unit. But in the 1950s that huge cooling tower was rocket science.

Rose McGowan's beautiful old house which
she inherited from her adoptive mother.

We would often go to Yompay's on hot summer afternoons to buy five cents worth of candy and just linger in the store as long as they would let us, enjoying the cool.

*

Another time when I went to her store on a quick errand before school, and after serving me, Rose reached deep into the freezer and came out with a near-empty, I mean *near-empty*, industrial-size container of strawberry ice cream. By the time I got home the ice cream was melting fast. When I scraped the sides and bottom, I discovered there were almost two scoops left in there. Before she gave me the container, Rose looked around furtively to make sure no one was watching. "Now don't you tell anyone, okay." she admonished me in a stern voice. You see, she didn't want anyone to see her giving gifts, even negligible things, because that might draw attention to her wealth. People could become envious.

I couldn't think of a secret I would rather keep — that I got to eat free strawberry ice cream for breakfast that day.

No problem, Raws! Mummm's the word!

VISIT TO THE REULET HOMESTEAD

Bonjour Les Cousins

Our direct Reulet ancestor, Bertrand, immigrated to the U.S. in 1842 and settled in Vacherie. He married a local girl, Arthemise Falgoust, and spent the rest of his life as a schooteacher in our little town, raising a large family. He died in 1876. From family lore we knew he had come from France but that's all we knew about him. When Uncle Lewis Reulet was in the U.S. Air Force and stationed in France in the early 1950s, he located Bertrand's family and paid them a visit. When I was in the U.S. Army in Germany in the mid 1960s, I also visited the Reulet homestead in May, 1967. Below is the account I sent home.

The first leg of my trip to the Reulets took me to Paris where I spent several days exploring that wonderful city, and spent some great times with a French friend who is stationed in the French army on the same base as me. But then my thoughts soon turned to the South and my upcoming visit to the Reulet family in Villeneuvre-Lecussan, a small settlement situated in the foothills of the Pyrenees Mountains.

To avoid rush hour traffic, I left Paris early in the morning, and drove the whole way on the Nationale 20, an old roman road that runs from Paris to Toulouse, a distance of almost 700 kilometers. Occasionally I stopped for coffee or to get a bite or to see a site of interest, but it was a long haul, and by the time I arrived in Toulouse, 12 hours later, all I wanted was a meal, a room, and a good night's sleep!

While having dinner at a small café next to my hotel, I checked the local phone directory and found four Reulets listed, debated whether to call, and finally decided against it, reasoning that they were probably of no relation to our country cousins, and in any case would not have been aware of my impending visit. I was also unsure if I could get across on the telephone with my Vacherie French. Later I discovered that one of the Reulets listed in that directory was actually a daughter of our branch of the family and had been with her folks in the country anticipating my arrival for the previous four days! So, it's possible my hesitancy about calling strangers cost me a good evening of genuine French hospitality.

After a restful night and a generous *petit-déjeuner* of *café-au-lait* and French bread with salted butter, I left Toulouse around 9:00 a.m., ready to face whatever the fates would throw at me. Considering the long drive of the previous day, I was in great form and high spirits.

It was a spring day in full bloom, the air crisp and refreshing, the countryside rich in vegetation. All around there were lovely views of small farms, vineyards, and rolling hills. For most of the morning heading west, the highway paralleled the Pyrenees along the banks of the Garonne River, a large waterway that drains the northern watershed of the Pyrenees and empties into the Atlantic Ocean near Bordeaux.

At one point on my journey, I stopped to sew a button on my blazer jacket, using my army kit. I had decided to wear proper dress clothes, because I thought that was how the Reulets would expect their *cousin américain* to be dressed.

It was mid-morning when I reached Montrejeau, the largest town in the area. I left the main road and headed north toward Villeneuvre-Lécussan, approximately five kilometres away, where the Reulet homestead was located.

Just off the highway, I found myself in real back country. The land was hilly and wooded with occasional patches of cultivation. Livestock roamed freely on the one-lane road, and I found myself feeling relieved it was hard-surfaced at least.

Villeneuvre was easy to find, being the only village in the area. I stoppod at a café for information and was told that the Reulet family lived "out of town" — if such a condition could be said to exist there. To me, even this tiny village was "out of town!"

The café owner directed me down a gravel road which wound over and around craggy hills, through small farms and homesteads. But there was no sign of our *cousins français* for miles, so I stopped again to ask for directions, this time from a lady doing her washing in the yard, using a tree stump for a washboard. She shook her head *No*, answering my query in an unintelligible shout, before turning to yell at a half-naked youngster who'd scurried up to her during our exchange. At that point, they both started to scream at me, or so it seemed. I couldn't make out a word of what they were trying to tell me; it sounded like they were speaking a patois. But whatever they were saying it didn't sound good, and for a minute I considered getting the hell out of there. But being an "old" Army man (with all of 13 months of service behind me), *my sense of mission was stronger than my sense of self-preservation*, as they say, so I continued my search.

A short time later, I came upon another homestead with a white frame and stone house, well built and sturdy looking, situated beside a small stream over which a sawmill was perched. Unlike the house, the sawmill appeared to be in an advanced state of disrepair. From what Uncle Lewis had told me, I figured this must be the home of Eloi Reulet, cousin Auguste's brother, who ran a sawmill when Lewis was there 13 years previously.

I went to the door and knocked, but no one answered. The search for my French relatives was becoming quite a formidable affair. But having come this far, I was determined not be discouraged and continued to drive all over this region of southern French "back country," looking for the Reulets.

Finally, I came upon a group of young boys playing in some trees. I stopped and asked for *La maison de la famille Auguste Reulet* (pronounced, "Reu-LAY" in France.) They scampered down, hopped onto their bikes, and took off down the road yelling over their shoulders, "Suivez-nous." ("Follow us.")

After a few hundred yards we came to an old farm house, the gate wide open. They indicated this was the place, so I drove through the gate and right up to the front door. (In truth, I was wary of the barking dogs.) My arrival was apparently observed from within, for no sooner had I knocked than the door flew open. It was Auguste's wife, Julie, who welcomed me warmly and invited me inside.

We exchanged the usual get-acquainted pleasantries, recalling Uncle Lewis's visit of 13 years before. I had no difficully understanding her or communicating in my Louisiana French. Julie said they'd been eagerly awaiting my visit and had kept a daily lookout for me after receiving my letter.

In fact, they had begun to worry that I might never show up at all.

At one point, Julie told me that her husband, Auguste, was in bed in the next room, gravely ill. She described his sickness as something that sounded to me like cancer. Then she suggested we go in and see him, but I demurred, trying to persuade her to leave him in peace. I didn't want to excite him too much and risk having him die in my presence. But Julie insisted, saying that he, too, had been fervently looking forward to my arrival, and it would do him good to see me. I relented, and we entered the room.

From our 1972 visit: Mama, Cousin Julie, our friend Marshall, and me. The original Reulet homestead in background, 200 years old at the time.

Apparently, Auguste overheard our conversation because when I approached, he stuck out a feeble hand in greeting. At first, I had difficulty understanding him; his illness had greatly affected his breath and his speech was strained. He spoke in gasps, and I got more nervous for him with his every word because it looked like speaking was demanding far too much energy. But he *wanted* to talk, and eventually I noticed that he started to regain some of his strength in the process, his breath becoming stronger and his voice more comprehensible. We spoke about the family, of course, the farm, the house, Lewis's visit in 1954, the Vacherie Reulets, my time in the military and so on, for at least half an hour. At one point, he proudly pointed out a framed medal that had been bestowed upon him for his service in WWI, now sitting in its place of honor on the mantlepiece.

*1972,
me and Marshall
helping bring in the
hay, cousin Jean
supervising.*

Julie, who had been in the kitchen preparing lunch, came into the bedroom and announced the arrival of their son, Jean. I took leave of the old man — he'd had just about all the talking he could handle for one day, I thought — and went out to meet Jean.

Jean, about 35, was just returning home from work. *Outside* work, that is — away from the farm. He was the first one in the family who had ever "worked away," spending his mornings toiling in an aluminum foundry nearby and working the farm in the afternoons. That had permitted the family to buy a few modern conveniences, one being a second-hand Peugeot automobile, which Jean proudly showed me. My 1959 Mercedes-Benz, however dusty and road-weary, greatly impressed him — a confirmation of my *riche cousin américain* status, I guess.

We sat down to lunch, and what a lunch it was. They were prepared to give me everything in their larder to ensure that I had an unforgettable meal. The feast began in the the proper French manner with the *apéritif*, a before-dinner drink, "Pour ouvrir l'appetit!" as Julie said. "To open the appetite!" They served a local traditional drink called *pastis* — a licorice-tasting alcoholic beverage cut with water and served over ice, which gives it a yellowish, cloudy aspect. Now in truth, licorice is a flavor I have never liked, so after my first sip I knew *pastis* was not for me and had to ask Jean for something else. Jean then poured me a local *vin cuit* ("cooked wine") which is a rather sweet cordial similar to port. This was much more to my liking and it went down well.

Next came the *entrée*: *paté* and *saussison* (cured sausage), eaten with freshly-baked bread from the local baker. The bread was made frome flour from the Reulets' wheat crop of the previous year. Jean explained that, while most of the wheat they grew was sold in the local market, a portion was set aside to be deliverd monthly to the baker, who in return gave them loaves of bread every day in a quantity commensurate with the value of the wheat. The family was provided with fresh bread twice daily, which they picked up at the *boulangerie,* and no money changed hands.

After that delicious entrée, we had a main course of *confit d'oie* (preserved goose), a special delicacy in those parts. It was served with Brussels sprouts, and I need not mention that the goose and sprouts were washed down with the best wines from the family casks for you to appreciate the gustatory treat that was mine that day.

At one point during the meal, Auguste came hobbling out of his room on a cane and took his place at the head of the table. According to Julie, it was the first time he had been on his feet in over two weeks. He did not eat very much but drank his share of wine. *"It's good for him!"* Julie assured me.

1972, checking what's for lunch, from left Cousin Julie, Marshall, Jude, Mama.

Next came the salad: crunchy lettuce with a rich mustard-based *vinaigrette,* followed by a selection of local cheeses, including a tasty variety made from goats' milk.

Coffee and cognac were served at the end of this splendid feast, followed by a very strong clear liquor Jean called *fil de fer* ("barbed wire" is a close translation). Julie had made that herself from plums grown on their land, and we sipped it straight, out of tiny glasses.

After dinner, Auguste insisted I accompany him to the *cave* (wine cellar) where he showed me several barrels and innumerable bottles of wine, as well as cheeses, sausages and about five cured hams hanging from low rafters — all, of course, homemade. It was obvious he took great pride in these products, and he tried to explain the various processes that went into the creation of each one, but it demanded great physical effort for him to speak. That said, he made a valiant attempt to be hospitable, even in his weakened condition, and I could see how much pleasure it gave him.

After lunch, Jean and I went out to try to find his uncle Eloi, but he was still not home, so we went to the fields where Jean presumed Eloi and his wife would be taking the cows out to pasture. Unable to find him there either, Jean decided to check with Eloi's son, a carpenter who was building a house in the area.

We soon located him. He was about Jean's age and his name was also Jean, so to distinguish him from "our" Jean, he was called, "Jean l'Artisan" (Jean the Craftsman). He wasn't certain of his father's whereabouts, so the three of us, joined by a friend of theirs, returned to the house to enjoy a final drink before the end of my short visit.

It was after five in the afternoon when I decided to be on my way, ignoring the pleas that I spend the night and even several days. I didn't want to ruin what was a very pleasant and memorable visit by getting involved in the problems of daily family life, with Auguste on his last legs. And secondly, I had a lot of territory to cover if I wanted to make it to the French Riviera, Italy and Austria in the remaining ten days of my leave. I promised to write, and perhaps visit again the following year before shipping back to the U.S. It had been wonderful to glimpse their simple, happy and uncluttered lives.

EULOGIES

UNCLE LEWIS REULET
(1927-2011)

Good morning, everyone, and welcome to Lewis Reulet's memorial.

If each one of us is special in his or her our own way, then Uncle Lewis was someone just *extra* special.

For one thing, he was the perfect dinner companion and the best person to take along on a long car ride, because there was never a dull conversational moment with him.

His interests ranged far and wide. He was a voracious reader, mostly history and biography, and had traveled the world as a young man in the Merchant Marines and the Air Force.

All of you know how droll and amusing he was. You laughed at his funny stories, made even more entertaining by his joke-telling style, which was second to none. But more than that, he was "*spirituel*" in the French sense: brilliantly mischievous. You never left his company without a desire to be with him again soon.

Of course, that in itself may not be so extraordinary; we all know many people who have some of these qualities. But what made Lewis so special, so endearing, was that there was something of the artist in him. The worldly and mundane could be put off until tomorrow; he marched to the beat of his own drum. And that beat was more often than not opera.

"*Rosa*" + *Lewis*   10/2 4/4

Uncle Lewis behind Rosa, getting the winter garden
ready for planting.

Part of what made Lewis so special was his passion for (and encyclopedic knowledge of) the operatic world — a dimension of his personality that casual acquaintances, and even some longtime friends, were not usually aware of. I think his interest in opera said more than anything about his intellectual sensibilities. He was an "*artiste*" in the full sense of the word.

But why opera? I always wondered where his musical proclivities came from; there had to have been some early influences. It was a mystery to me because coming from the culturally deprived Vacherie of the 1930s and '40s, I figured he couldn't have been exposed to much music early on, except perhaps the St. James High School marching band!

Well, I was wrong. A few years ago, on a ride to Livonia, west of Baton Rouge, to have lunch at Joe Major's place, the conversation turned to music and I asked him, "Why opera?" He proceeded to enlighten me on a subject that was dear to him.

It seems that when Lewis was growing up, the Metropolitan Opera of New York had a program on the radio every Saturday afternoon, *Live from the Met*. (I checked, and it's still going strong after 70-plus years on the air.) The broadcast was carried by the only station of any consequence in New Orleans, WWL. Every Saturday, following the midday news, the Met came on *live* for a three-hour program.

Lewis gradually started looking forward to his Saturday afternoon opera session. But it was not yet a deep passion, perhaps because he had neither records to listen to nor friends to share his interest with. Then one day when Lewis was in his early teens, Pépère Victor had a carpenter come to the house to work on the cisterns (Pépère had four — FOUR! — huge wooden cisterns — the Reulets were not about to run out of water!)

The carpenter was Jean Waguespack, a bachelor from Front Vacherie — and apparently not the cultural backwater Back Vacherie was then. Jean was an opera buff and very knowledgeable about the genre. Mémère fixed them lunch and while they ate, the Met broadcast came on the radio. Jean told Lewis all about his love of opera and his favorite singers, and that was the eureka moment for Lewis — the moment he found someone who not only shared his interest, but was well informed on the subject, too.

The next day, Jean came to work bearing a few opera records — those old, scratchy 78s (Aunt Janice remembers one being of Enrico Caruso). They played them on the crank-up gramophone in the living room, with commentary from Jean. From that day on, Lewis was a goner for opera.

*

Lewis was also known in the family as the one who "found" the Reulets in France (although they always maintained they were not "lost"). While in the Air Force in the early 1950s, after some time in Germany, he was posted in France, which was a dream come true for him. Stationed in Chateauroux, in the center of the country, for about two years, he got the idea that maybe he could find the Vacherie Reulet ancestors. He wrote his mother, Mémère Hélène, asking for some information. "If you know the names of our Reulet cousins in France, I might be able to find out something about them."

She sent him the information she had, and he wrote to various town halls in areas the Reulets were thought to have come from. Eventually, he located them and made the first of many pilgrimages to the original Reulet homestead members of the family would make over the next 50 years.

After 42 years away, Lewis came back to visit France in 1996. He spent a few days with us in Paris, and then headed on down south, first to stop in Chateauroux to try to contact some old friends, and then to the Reulets. He had his little black book with him from his time in the service — it actually *was* <u>little</u> and <u>black</u> — and after a few days' search, he found one old friend who put him in touch with a few more.

One of them was Madeleine Chalumeau (Cha–lu—meau), an old "flame" (more on this word later) from his Air Force days, who was widowed and living in the area. They had a happy reunion, and then he went on to visit the Reulets down south. On the way back to Paris, he decided to make an unscheduled stop in Chateauroux — to tell Madeleine good bye, I imagine. (He was nothing if not "canaille," that Lewis.)

We had a great time with him that last week in Paris. We went to the opera, of course, met many musicians from the orchestra, and dined with friends around town. Every time I introduced Lewis, I'd say that he had just reconnected with friends from long ago, and I never omitted to pronounce Madeleine's last name loud and clear, "Cha-lu-meau." That always elicited smiles and giggles because the word *chalumeau* means "blow torch" in French. People would start joking, "Bet she was HOT!" Or: "And you made it back to Paris ALIVE?"

The last time I saw him, this past May, we joked about Miss Blow Torch again and had a good laugh.

We won't be seeing the likes of Lewis again soon; he was truly unforgettable.

UNCLE WOOD REULET
(1919 – 2014)

Good morning, and a warm welcome to the Missouri contingent — Aunt Rita's family — who came so far to be with us.

I had a more personal relationship with Uncle Wood than most of you here today: he was my *parrain* (godfather, for the Missourians who may not know that word). And how that came about is a *Woodsian* kind of story.

As the good pastor told you a few moments ago, Wood was a headstrong individual; he went right to the point whatever it was. In fact, he could be downright brusque, which, when you loved him, you regarded as part of his charm, although his "suggestions" were not always readily welcomed by others. But in this particular story, he took a more, should we say, "diplomatic" approach...

Wood was home on a furlough from the Army in early June of 1942, the very week I was born. He wanted to be chosen as my *parrain*, and when he realized that my birth was fast approaching, he decided to plead his case to Aunt Florence — the oldest of the Reulet children, and the wisest, according to pretty much everyone. Even Pépère Victor always went down the road to consult with her when he had a major decision to take.

Wood went to see Florence and asked her to intervene with Mama on his behalf. Of course, there were no telephones back then, so he had to drive Florence up the road to the Reulet homestead so she could speak with Mama.

And the day after I was born, he and Tante Elise took me to church to be baptized and became my godparents.

Some time later, when Wood was stationed in the Pacific, he sent us a $25 War Bond in my name, which I realized later must have been a great sacrifice for him, given the paltry pay servicemen got at the time. The Bond was put in the strongbox at the bank, and it was not until 22 years later that I cashed it. I called him in Baton Rouge to thank him. He had completely forgotten about it, because by that time he had a gang of kids of his own to worry about. (That gang is here with us today, sitting in the front row.)

Uncle Wood in Missouri before shipping out to the Pacific.

*

When Elton Oubre and I went to see Wood a few years ago at the Veterans' Retirement Home in Jackson, Louisiana, (for the Missourians, Jackson is also the home of the Louisiana Hospital for the Mentally Deranged), he was very happy to have our visit and told us, "You know, all the people in Jackson are not crazy — and all the crazy people are not in Jackson." That was a popular saying in Vacherie, and still is.

Knowing Wood's penchant for running things, telling people what should be done and how, when he entered the Veterans' home, I told Team Reulet (as we call our little traveling and eating club: Janice, Marjorie, Lael and me) that with Wood installed in the VA home, the director would have to be placed on administrative leave as Wood would have the place humming in no time.

We always joked about that when we talked about Uncle Wood being at the VA Home. So, when Lael called earlier this week to inform us of his passing, I reminded her that the other director of the VA home should now be invited back to assume his former duties, since the directorship position was now vacant.

Thank you, and wishing a pleasant stay in Baton Rouge to our friends from Missouri.

HELEN GRAVOIS OBIT

(THE TIMES-PICAYUNE)

(Note: this short obituary was distributed in the church for the funeral services.)

Helen Eugenie Reulet Gravois, a noted local historian and linguist, died of natural causes on May 29, 2009, at the age of 93. She was a native and life-long resident of Vacherie.

She was considered by many to be the person to go to as far as local historical events and family histories were concerned. She possessed an extraordinary memory and very much enjoyed relaying information and telling stories from the past. Both friends and strangers, who would soon become her friends, would call on her for tidbits of detailed information. She once had her picture in the New York Times for an article on Vacherie. Genealogists from throughout the area often visited her to obtain hard-to-find information.

Mrs. Helen had outstanding linguistic abilities, both in English and in French. For several decades, her weekly column Le Coin Français (The French Corner) was enjoyed by readers of *The Enterprise* and *The News-Examiner*. In her column, she gave English translations of commonly used French words and sayings. She was often called upon for the correct spelling, definition and usage of particular French words and phrases. She periodically wrote articles for the local papers on growing up in Vacherie and the days gone by. She was a believer and promoter to her family and others of the value of education. A 1932 graduate of St. James High School, she went to college beginning in 1960, 28 years after finishing high school (and after marrying and raising her family). She obtained a degree from Nicholls State University at the tender age of 49, and graduated on the same day as her older son, Colin. She went on to have a distinguished career as an elementary school librarian before retiring and enjoying a happy retirement with her husband until his death.

She enjoyed reading, writing and traveling, especially to visit her son Colin and his family in Paris, and her Reulet cousins in southern France. She went to France and Europe 13 times in the past 37 years, the last time just a few years before her death.

As a result of her service and involvement in the community, Mrs. Helen was the recipient of the 1998 "Good Citizen of the Year" award presented by *The Enterprise*.

Please join the family for a reception in the Church Hall following the funeral services.

HELEN EUGENIE REULET GRAVOIS
(1915-2009)

Good morning, and thank you all for coming. Looking at all the people in the church this morning, I see friends and relatives from all over South Louisiana, from Texas and Florida, and Mama's dear friend Kathleen from New York. Mama would be embarasscd by all the fuss being made over her since last Friday, she was so modest. But today is her day, and she'll just have to accept it.

A few years ago, on one of our rides around the area (and, oh, how she loved to go on rides), at the time when she began, I imagine, to see the shadows lengthening, and realized that she would not be with us forever, she turned to me and said: "When the time comes and I'm no longer with you all, could you say a few words about me?"

That time has come today.

I'm not going to stand here and tell you how good she was, or how caring, loving, generous, how kind she was. You all know that already, that's why you're here. I'll just try to shine a little light on a few aspects of her long and full life.

Helen Eugenie Reulet was born in Vacherie on November 7, 1915, on the Back Lane, "up the road" as they called it (or "en haut" as they really called it), 93 years and seven months ago. She was the fifth of 13 children born to Victor Reulet and Helen Poirier, and was named after her mother and her grandmother, Eugenie.

Mama was born in a house directly across the road from the house she lived in for the last 60 years of her life. Over the past few years, and especially when she was more and more confined to the house, she'd sit in her chair and look out across the road to the place where she was born and relive those days of yesteryear.

The conversation never failed to come back to her father, Victor, or Papa, as she called him, and to Aunt Marie, Victor's sister. She always said they were the most important influences in her life. She never took a major decision without consulting them.

Victor was a loving and caring father, and in his job as a traveling salesman, he often took some of his children with him on sales trips all over southeastern Louisiana. That's probably where Mama got her urge to see the wider world. She would often lament the fact that trans-Atlantic jet travel came 10 years too late for Victor to go to Europe. How he would have loved to see France, she would say, and how he would have loved to visit with the Reulets on the original home place.

Well, I guess she had to make up for what he missed because she traveled to France, with sidetrips to Greece, Italy, England, North Africa and other places, 13 times in the past 37 years, the last time when she was 89 years young.

In 1919, when Mama was four years old, they went to live at Valcour Aime, a plantation about seven miles from Back Vacherie, where her father Victor wanted to try his hand at sugarcane farming. The family was growing, and he felt that would be an opportunity to make more money. He rented some acreage and moved the family to the river.

Unfortunately, after a few years, blight hit the sugarcane in this area and he lost his investment. But what's germane to our story here is that Mama started school while they were at Valcour Aime. On her first day, she cried uncontrollably for hours, "wailed" she said, because they were speaking a foreign language she didn't understand (English). Pépère decided to let her sit out the year. So, she stayed home with Mémère and the young ones — a ironic beginning for someone who later prized education so much. She soon caught up with her classmates her age when she skipped second grade, and all was well again.

So, Pépère Victor moved the family back to Vacherie, and they lived in several houses for a short time in the Front Lane, then moved back to the original house where Mama had been born — Uncle Gus's house — which they rented. They stayed there until 1934 when Pépère built a house of their own, the one Marjorie lives in today.

Mama's two older sisters, Florence and Mae, finished high school in 1929 and '30, and went on to college in Lafayette. Mama graduated from high school in 1932, the first class to finish in the new school, that beautiful three-story brick building we all loved so much which burned down a few years ago. She was hoping to go to college after high school, like her sisters. But unfortunately, the country was in the depths of the Depression that year, and no way could be found to finance a higher education. So, she stayed home, helping Mémère with the younger ones, her dream of college seemingly still-born.

Little did she know...

Fast-forward to 1939. In September of that year, she married our father, Jean Paul Gravois. He was a younger brother of Florence's husband, Antoine. So, all those visits down the road to the Gravois house for her, or up the road to the Reulet house for him, and then up the road, down the road, and up and down the road again, led naturally to the blooming of a romance. And that's how we became double first cousins with Florence and Antoine's brood.

Just a few years earlier, her sister Mae had married a Gravois cousin, Gaston, so pretty soon there were so many little and big Reulet and Gravois people running around the place that we practically didn't realize there were any other kind of people in the world.

Our parents' first house was in Front Vacherie. They settled into marital bliss in the old Smith place, a sturdy red brick building on the Vacherie Road. Lael was born there in 1941. Less than a year later, they returned to the Back, and lived with Mémère and Pépère for some months to save rent money while they built a house in the yard between Pépère and Aunt Marie. Mama gave birth to me in that house in June, 1942.

Fast forward to August, 1947. We are on a short vacation to Grand Isle, several vehicles transporting some 15 or so happy campers. (Actually, we didn't camp out! We stayed in Uncle Prudent and Aunt Rosemary's tourist cabins.) Most of us young ones rode in the back of Uncle Philip's delivery truck with a tarp for protection from the sun and rain.

It was a wonderful, exciting ride. It was as if we were going to the ends of the earth because no one took vacations then.

Many years later, Mama told me that after passing Thibodaux on the road to Grand Isle, she noticed some major construction on what was then Acadia Plantation. She wondered out loud what it was, and Daddy told her he had heard that LSU was building a junior college in the area and perhaps that was the construction site. She said she thought to herself at the time, *if only my children could have the opportunity to go to college there.*

Little did she know...

The 1940s came to an end and the '50s saw a rapidly expanding family. Mary was born in 1949, Margaret came in 1951, and then Jude in 1953, which made for a family of five children with Lael and me.

Lael and me on the beach in Grand Isle, behind us cousin Jimmie Steib, 1947.

Fast forward to 1960. I finished high school at the end of May, and after a few days looking over the situation (it was very hot, no airconditioning then, and no part-time jobs for students available in the Vacherie area), I decided to enter college in June instead of waiting for the fall semester. That turned out to be a very auspicious decision, as you will soon see. Or said another way: Nothing happens in a vacuum.

A few days after summer classes began, I returned to the house one evening to find Mama seated at the kitchen-table looking over my books and school papers. When she saw me, she motioned me to come sit with her for a few minutes; she had a few things to ask me.

"What books are these — your class books or some books you are just reading?"

I told her they were the textbooks for the courses I was taking, and she answered, "Why, I know all that."

I replied, a bit smart alecky, that I wasn't surprised, as she was much older than me, but she answered, cryptically, "That's just the point." We left it at that.

Not more than a week later she asked me, "Would it bother you if I started college in September and rode the same bus as you?"

"Uh...uh...no, not really..." I answered. However, I really didn't think that was going to happen.

But the idea germinated in her mind, and one Sunday at the end of July, she asked me to go with her to Aunt Marie's that afternoon to see what Marie thought about it; she needed to get her on board.

We sat on the front porch in the old rockers, rocking away, watching the cars pass as we talked, as was our usual custom. Mama waited for a propitious moment in the conversation, and then she popped it on Aunt Marie. Aunt Marie almost had conniptions,

"Mais jamais, Nell, mais jamais, t'es trop vieille pour faire ça. "

No, no, Nell," (Marie used the name Mama's family always called her.) "You're way too old for that."

But after a while, Aunt Marie came around to appreciate Mama's determination and the logic of her plan, and finally gave it her blessing.

"Well, yes, do it. If you don't give it a try, you'll regret it for the rest. of your life." She was a very wise woman, Aunt Marie was.

Daddy was also dead set against the idea, as would be expected from someone his age and station in life. He said, like Aunt Marie, that Mama was too old, that she had enough to do at home with the housework and the children and keeping him happy. He was also probably wondering what his friends would say about that "old woman" going to school with the young college kids. But eventually, he came around, too, and was soon on board. Has any man been known to resist a determined woman — and win?

Now she had Aunt Marie and Daddy on board, but she still needed some moral support; after all that was 1960 — older people going to college was something just not done then, at least not in the rural setting we were part of. These days, it's common to see human interest stories in the papers and on television about the 83-year~old grandmother finally getting her college degree, or the 92-year-old twins graduating *cum laude* from some university or other. But we're talking 1960 Vacherie here, we're not talking human interest. We're talking life goals! This was serious!

So, she enlisted a friend to go with her, Angelina Falgoust (wife of the school bus driver, Louis Falgoust) who also, as a young woman, had harbored dreams of going to college and had not been able to do so at the time. Soon she and Angelina were meeting almost daily at our house, planning their college

With Mama in a Paris café reading "Le Monde",
June 2003.

career. (Perhaps Angelina's husband was not yet aware of the goings-on.) They were as excited as two young freshman girls about to embark on life's big adventure.

And so, September arrived, and we were driving to Thibodaux with Angelina in tow, but on the way she started to backslide. Mama encouraged her with some soothing words, and Angelina took her courage in hand, and in they went to register. I don't remember if Angelina completed registration and paid the fees or not, but in any case, she declared the next day that she could not go through with it. Mama was sorry for her, but once she got her own foot in the door, it was no looking back. And so she began her college career.

She had been out of high school 28 years, she was 44 years old, with three children in elementary school, but she was detemined to succeed, and she sailed through the next four years, including summer sessions and some night classes, balancing her wifely and motherly duties with the rigors of scholarship, and it went off without a hitch.

Every morning she took the bus at 7:30, after getting her husband and children off to work and school, spent the whole day on campus, returned home at 4:30 in the afternoon, helped the children with their homework, cooked dinner, cleaned up afterwards, did the washing, the ironing, took care of Daddy's spiritul and temporal needs, did her homework after everyone was safely in bed — and then started the same routine all over again the next morning at six o'clock. Never did she complain, never did she say she was tired; she just did what she had to do to get what she wanted.

I figured out after a semester or two what her secret was: wise time management, while we young college kids (in full hormonal bloom) spent time between classes chasing the girls, playing chess, screwing around in the student center, getting a beer at the College Inn. Well, she had already done all that so she spent her free time quietly in a corner of the student center or an empty classroom, where she did most of her homework and studying. She was then free at night to attend to her family. Weekends, she did both.

One time at Aunt Marie's, it was a few days before the summer session would begin, her cousin Maybelle was sitting on the front porch with us. It was a hot afternoon like those summer days of 'yore. Maybelle said, "Nell, you must be tired. Why don't you stay home and rest this summer and spend it with us under the pecan trees, like we used to do?" Mama told Maybelle that, on the contrary, she was having the time of her life — was not at all tired, that "tired" was only a relative concept for her, and it was all just a lot of fun. She also said, "Maybelle, did you ever hear of someone skipping a football game because

*Mama, me, Jimmy Shuman, Hamida having lunch
in the Loire Valley, July 2003.*

they were a little tired? Well, this is my football game." Mama could tell it like it was.

Finally, the big day came around, and we graduated together, me before her, as we went by alphabetical order, which permitted me to tease her that I was smarter than she was. But the person most proud was Daddy. I guess he had won bragging rights with his friends; in fact, he began to take the credit for urging her to go to college. She knew then it had been the right decision.

But she was not finished, far from it. She took a job teaching third grade at Vacherie Elementary and loved it. But soon she got the idea that one day they would build a library at the school, and maybe, just maybe, who knows...

So she went back to college during the summers and took night classes to get a degree in library science, and about the time she got certified, the school built a library and she became the librarian — a job she held until her retirement at 67. She said she just loved every minute of her college and working career.

During her retirement, she had more time to travel around the country and to France, but she also continued with some night classes or, now and then, a summer session. She wanted to keep up with what was going on in her profession.

She also loved to take long rides visiting family and friends around south Louisiana. Every time I'd come back for a visit, we'd make a list of where she wanted to go. First of all, it was to see Aunt Mae in New Orleans, that was always the first thing, and also visit the Rodrigue and Marse cousins uptown on Henry Clay. We went to see Ernest and Deanna Freyou in New Iberia and have lunch with them in Franklin. We rediscovered "lost" Reulet cousins in Grosse Tete. We saw her brothers and their families in Baton Rouge. We lunched at Nobile's in Lutcher where she was always happy to see Wilbur Reynaud, her "boss," as she called him, the publisher of the *News-Examiner,* and the editor, Huey Stein. And we never forgot to visit with Audrey George in Houma. She always said, "Audrey — mais ça c'est une Madame!" ("Now Audrey — what a lady!").

My parents Helen and Paul in Vacherie, France, 1990.
Note the cows in the pasture, a "vacherie" of sorts.

She loved working on her regular column, "The French Corner," in the local weekly's. She was always busy researching one thing or another to put in the paper. She also wrote many stories about days gone by.

But what she loved most of all was the company of lively and interesting people. She loved to discuss the issues of the

Mama at the News-Examiner office correcting proofs on one of her stories, with Hamida and the editor Huey Stein.

day, the history of Vacherie and St. James, events of the past. Two people who were among the brightest stars in her galaxy were Huey Stein and Elton Oubre. When Huey became editor of both local papers, they had many things to talk about, and he sometimes went to her for advice or background on stories he was writing. Of course, when Elton came out with his book on Vacherie, well, his star went into orbit.

Huey passed away a few years ago, too soon for us all, and one day Mama said she really wished he were still with us — she had a few things she would have wanted to discuss with him. She took a deep contemplative breath, sighed, and said, "Well, we lost Huey, okay. But don't forget, we still have Elton." That's just the way she was.

She loved to have people sup at her table, and these past few years I frequently organized dinners at home with friends she would like to see, and every time, just before the guests started to arrive, when she came into the living room, all, *"pomponnéed and farode"* as they used to say, she'd invariably tell me, "I don't care where you place me at the table tonight; just make sure it's next to Elton. I have a few things I want to discuss with him." That's just the way she was.

A few days before Christmas two years ago, we came home one afternoon from a long ride and found a package for her at the door. Someone had passed and left it in our absence. It was a book on the history of the French language from our dear friend, Larry Becnel. Mama said we have to call to thank him, and I said, not necessary at the moment because in a few days we would be seeing him at a Forum get-together at D.J.'s restaurant, and she could thank him in person. "Oh, good," she said — one of her favorite expressions.

On the day of the dinner, when I came home to pick her up, she was busy at her desk with Larry's book, marking pages, underlining passages, taking notes. I remarked that she must be enjoying the book very much to be poring over it so carefully. But she told me, "You said we're going to see Larry tonight. I want to be prepared in case he asks me a question." She was 91 years old then. That was just the way she was.

I guess I'm running out of time; Father Mike right here is getting a little nervous. I was told to keep it short, five, ten minutes max (I'm cheating a bit, Father!), so just this final thing. It was December, 2000, a nice warm sunny day, and we went for a ride downriver to Luling, across the bridge, then back upriver on the East Bank before having lunch in Donalsonville, and back home. It was a long ride, a full day, and it was Daddy's last outing before he took to bed with his final illness. Lael and Hamida were with us. We took the river road all the way, the "scenic" one, the one we used to take to get to New Orleans before the Interstates and the new bridges made it all so easy.

The route took us through Edgard, Lucy and then Killona. This area was blighted since White flight and Black emigration had emptied it of almost everyone but poor African-Americans. There the gentlemen hung around in front of stores drinking their alcohol from brown paper bags. This was not a place that would normally bring pleasant thoughts. While we were passing in front of the old Soraparu Bar and Grocery, long since abandoned and in ruins, Mama suddenly said to no one in particular, "You know what the greatest thing to happen in my lifetime was?" In the few seconds between the question and the answer that was sure to follow, I thought, *Roosevelt? WWII? The moon landing?*

But she said only one word, "Integration." She chose that time and place, that particular uninviting locale, to make a strong personal statement. Other "normal" people of the same skin color as her, given the circumstances, would probably have said something completely opposite ("Country's going to ruins.") But she just wanted to let us know that a wrong had been righted, in her lifetime, and it was not open for discussion. That was just the way she was.

If we could draw a lesson from Mama's long and full life, it would be the following:

If you want something badly enough and you're willing to work hard, very hard, and not take "no" for an answer, then you can do it. Keep your eye on the prize!

And she did. Thank you.

ACKNOWLEDGEMENTS

I have many people to thank.

First, Jerry Schexnayder, for founding the Vacherie Forum blog where some of these stories, in slightly different form, first saw the light of day. Thank you, Jerry, for that outstanding accomplishment of helping preserve local history. I would be seriously remiss if I didn't express deep gratitude to my aunts Janice Reulet Daigle and Marjorie Reulet Granier for stories of Vacherie days before my time and especially for sharing memories of my grandfather Pépère Victor. I cannot forget my old Vacherie friends, Elton Oubre and Huey Stein, who are no longer with us. We told and retold many of these stories over the years — and they got better with the retelling. Sincere thanks to Marshall Leaffer and Jimmy Shuman, dear friends of over 50 years, who persuaded me to put these stories in writing and were nice enough not to stop me when they were hearing some for the umpteenth time. Kathleen Modrowski, one of my dearest friends, who always encouraged me to push on further in my many endeavors. She has been a singular inspiration for this book. E.J. Gilbert, Jr., for sharing stories of growing up straddling the color line in New Orleans, and for sending me a few photos to illustrate some stories.

The late Jim Haynes from Haynesville, Louisiana, a dear friend and long-time Parisian expat who inspired many people, including me, to follow their dreams.

Monique Wells for permission to quote in its entirety her blog post on the saga of my portrait painted by Beauford Delaney. Thanks, Monique. Pam Folse for the picture of Père Augustin Delnom.

Richard Allen, dear friend and fellow expat, whose stories of growing up in Harlem helped inform my understanding of the Black experience. And a special thank you to his late mother, Mary, for raising such a fine gentleman. I'm grateful to my editor par excellence, Mimi Seton, who helped me put these stories in better form, and teased meanings out of some of my words that I didn't know existed. (Any errors are my own.) Catherine Oubre Hymel, the present caretaker of the Mad Stone, for giving me a demonstration of its uses, and sending a great picture for the book. Dr. Leslie P. Theard, who over the years shared his experience of growing up in segregated New Orleans and enlightened me on the issues of navigating the subtle racial hurdles an executive of color faced in the upper echelons of the American corporate world. Thanks to Joe DeSalvo and Joanne Sealy, book people extraordinaire, from Faulkner House Books in New Orleans. Their wise counsel on the art of the memoir proved invaluable.

Julie Granier Borne for some additional photos when I realized I was missing a few. She diligently found what I needed and sent them to me pronto. Jerry Folse, who shared the story of his ancestor, Antoine Folse, and gave me some old maps of the area to help me better understand early Vacherie. Larry Becnel, noted lawyer and dear friend, who graciously shared over the years his deep knowledge of Louisiana and Vacherie history. Every time I write something in his area of expertise, I always ask myself: What would Larry say? My Vacherie pal Edward Charles Becnel for helping me download *at a distance,* from my Vacherie computer, the digital files and pictures for this book. I owe a special debt of gratitude to Gilles Arira, master book layout specialist, who ably steered me through the publishing process, and using my digital files produced the book you are holding in your hands. Merci beaucoup, Gilles.

Thanks to my daughter Hana, who assisted in research and choosing photos, and she took care of a lot of other tedious publishing chores while I was recovering from knee replacement surgery. Your help was precious. It could not have happened without you! I can't forget my daughter Kenza, who helped me find documents at the courthouse and assisted with interviews in Vacherie. She offered continuous words of encouragement from her home in Mexico City. And to my wonderful wife Hamida, who kept the ship on an even keel when I was consumed by this task. Thank you for not complaining when the work made me late for lunch or dinner. Truly, I could not have seen this project through to the end without you by my side.

I am deeply indebted to all of you.

Colin Gravois...Paris, France...27 December 2020

At the US Ambassador's July 4th picnic,
Paris 2012, from left me, Kenza, Hamida, and Hana.

Picture Gallery

Most of the old-time pictures in this book were taken by my mother, Helen. She used an inexpensive Kodak camera, given to her by Uncle Wood, which is the reason why some pictures are not too sharply focused, but we're still glad to have them. And that's also why she's practically never in the pictures; she was too busy taking them. She'd send the completed rolls of film off to Fox Studios in Fort Worth, Texas, and a few days later we'd get the pictures back in the mail. It was a good, cheap, and simple arrangement.

I'm putting some additional left-over photos in this Picture Gallery, each with its own story to tell, and also a few contemporary ones of dear friends. Sorry, I didn't have space for all of you. I would have had to add an additional hundred pages to the book to fit them all in! But remember, you all have a special place in my heart.

Cover photo. *Sunday outing at Uncle Tony's hunting camp on Lac des Allemands, 1946. I am in my favorite spot in the crook of Pépère's arm, lower right...*

The Gravois brothers, 1945, from left Leonard, my father Paul, Joe, Pépère Nénesse, Louis, Augustin. Absent Antoine.

Repairing Mémère's driveway with the help of Margaret, Mary, and Jude, 1956.

Giving a tired helper a lift in the wheelbarrow.

*With hoe in hand I'm preparing the garden
for spring planting, March 1957.*

*Guests at my parents' wedding reception. Janice
and Marjorie can surely identify most of them.
In background, right, Boy's house.*

Once in a lifetime event, 1957. Me with Mary, Mr. Snowman, Lael, Margaret, Jude.

Pépère gave me a calf for my birthday, 1946, and with it the task of caring and feeding it daily.

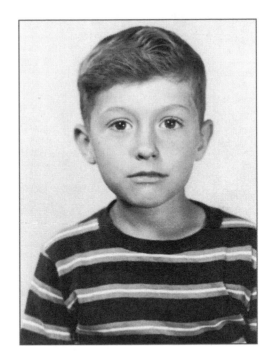

My second-grade school picture, 1950.

Hamida and me at the Laurel Valley plantation offices, 2010.

Papa Colin, sister Hana, and Mama Hamida welcoming home newly arrived Kenza, September 1983.

Easter vacation in Greece, Kenza was 7 months, Hana 3 years, April 1984.

All dressed up for a wedding: Pépère, Aunt Janice, Lael, and me.

Hamida on a spin on Lac des Allemands in our Vacherie neighbor Morrison Narcisse's boat.

*Dear friend Larry Becnel,
noted lawyer and historian.*

*The boys from Moonshine, La.,
Les Theard and Bébé Scioneaux.*

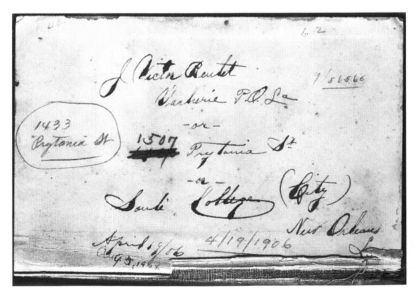

Some Pépère scribblings in one of his books.

*More Pépère scribblings, 1906. Apparently, there was a change
in street numbers on Prytania around that time.*

Posing for the camerawoman in front of our house:
Jude, me, Mary, Margaret, 1958.

Our favorite pilot Stayce Diamond Harris (Lt. Gen, USAF)
in the Pentagon Hall of Heroes.

*Showing off my zucchini
pickings in our garden
in France.*

*Dearest pal Jimmy Shuman,
fellow Paris expat and our
favorite actor and speaker.*

*My running-around pal
since 1969, Marshall Leaffer:
50-plus years, 4 continents,
and innumerable
gastronomic dinners.*

Dearest friend, Kathleen Modrowski, here in her "movie-star" days, Tunisia 1973.

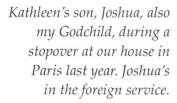

Kathleen's son, Joshua, also my Godchild, during a stopover at our house in Paris last year. Joshua's in the foreign service.

Richard Allen, fellow expat and dear friend,
and my number one chess pal over the years.

World citizen Jim Haynes, Louisiana native
and long-time Paris resident. We lost him
at the beginning of January 2021.

Our first skiing trip in the Alps at Val Thorens, December 1986. Hana was 5, Kenza 3.

Best neighbor in the world, Morrison Narcisse, and a true friend.

*Debbie Dixon with the Theard twins Les and
Lowell at their 85th birthday party in Paris.*

*Reveling in present company after a great lunch at our
favorite watering hole in Paris, La Closerie des Lilas,
with Jimmy Shuman and Marshall Leaffer.*

Vacherie's best: Auguste Baptist, master carpenter, with his longtime aide Lawrence Keller. Their restructuring and modernizing brought my family house into the 21ˢᵗ century.

France's greatest cellist and a very dear friend René Benedetti showing his stuff at one of our parties.

LOUISIANA

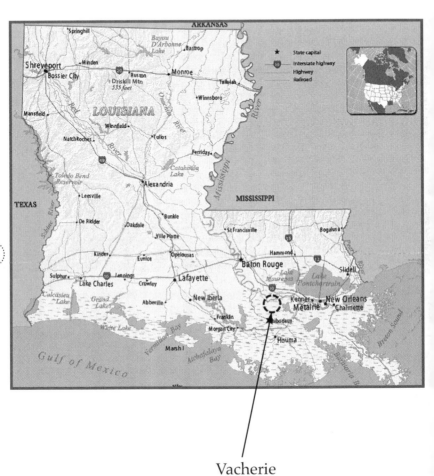

Vacherie

THE MISSISSIPPI DELTA

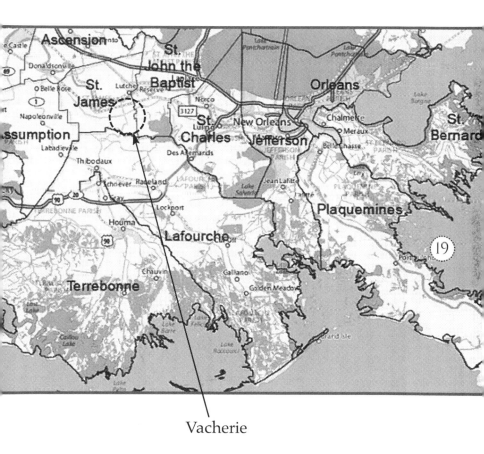

Vacherie

Vacherie in the Greater Mississippi Delta: rising sea levels coupled with land subsidence is wearing away approximately 25 to 35 square miles of land every year. The situation is becoming critical. The U.S. Army Corps of Engineers has just announced a 60-billion, 50-year plan to stabilize the state's southern littoral by diverting sediment-carrying Mississippi River waters to the delta zone. To quote The New Yorker: "Since the nineteen-thirties, Louisiana has shrunk by more than two thousand square miles. If Delaware or Rhode Island had lost that much territory, the U.S. would have only forty-nine states."

*Our dear friend and favorite crooner Bob Dockery belts
one out at one of our parties, with our house pianist
Victor Adelaide working his miracles on the keyboard.*

*With Marshall on one of our frequent Friday gastronomic day trips,
this one in Sancerre in the Upper Loire Valley at a 3-star restaurant
at top of the Sancerre hill overlooking the vineyards.
Doesn't get any better.*

Julie and Jerry Folse visiting with eminent civil rights lawyer Lolis Edward Elie on the patio of his house in the Tremé neighborhood of New Orleans.

Bubbly flowing: celebrating in the sun on the first day of Spring 2012, with Jimmy Shuman and Hamida.

With my sister Lael and Aunt Marjorie in Houma, La., in 2015 on a visit to our cousin Wilson Dugas. He was from Mémère Hélène's (Poirier) branch of the family.

My incomparable reading spot on the back sun-porch. Perfect diffused light for reading comfort.

Made in United States
Orlando, FL
03 April 2022